Rhett & Scarlett: The Lives and Legacies of Clark Gable and Vivien Leigh

By Charles River Editors

Studio shot of Clark Gable circa 1940

About Charles River Editors

Charles River Editors was founded by Harvard and MIT alumni to provide superior editing and original writing services, with the expertise to create digital content for publishers across a vast range of subject matter. In addition to providing original digital content for third party publishers, Charles River Editors republishes civilization's greatest literary works, bringing them to a new generation via ebooks.

Introduction

Clark Gable and Vivien Leigh in *Gone with the Wind*

Clark Gable (1901-1960)

"The only reason they come to see me is that I know that life is great — and they know I know it." – Clark Gable

The 1930s were, without a doubt, the height of the classical Hollywood era. It is no accident that 1939 has historically been designated as the pinnacle of Hollywood film history. The era was known for its lavish studio productions, with MGM, RKO, Warner Brothers, Paramount, and 20th Century Fox all operating at the height of their powers. Every major studio possessed a long roster of contract players, with films released at such a rapid pace that it made for an especially competitive environment within the industry. Even while America remained in the throes of the Great Depression, the film industry continued to flourish, and movies easily supplanted the theater as the main attraction for American entertainment. Indeed, it would be no exaggeration to claim that the film industry reached its zenith during the decade precisely because it offered an affordable (if very temporary) escape from the anxieties of the economic woes of the era.

The 1930s were also a time in which Hollywood boasted an unprecedented array of famous leading men. Gary Cooper, Cary Grant, James Stewart, and Fred Astaire were just a handful of the A-list stars of the decade, and it is in this context that the achievements of Clark Gable are particularly remarkable. Best known for his role in *Gone with the Wind* (1939), Gable reached the ranks of the Hollywood elite well before the end of the decade through acting in films such as *It Happened One Night* (1934) and *Mutiny on the Bounty* (1935). Gable had a unique appeal that captivated Depression-era audiences; while Cary Grant offered a sophisticated charm and Fred Astaire was tied to the musical genre, Gable brought an air of sophistication that was less comical than that of Grant and appealed to both genders, unlike Astaire. At a time when so many Americans were financially destitute, Gable managed to appear classy without coming across as snobbish. At the same time, his virile masculinity was not overly macho or misogynist. For these reasons, Gable was able to captivate male and female viewers alike, and his mass appeal was a driving force behind the commercial success of *Gone With the Wind*, possibly the most beloved Hollywood film ever made. As iconic director John Huston once stated, "Clark Gable was the only real he-man I've ever known, of all the actors I've met."

Even if Gable is perhaps less widely-known than Grant or Astaire among 21st century audiences, examining the effect he had on viewers during the 1930s and 1940s allows a better understanding of Hollywood during its Golden Age. In conjunction with that, his career served as a sort of response to his upbringing and cultural background. In fact, there was a significant gap between his glamorous roles on the movie screen and the real-life adversity he faced from an early age. Gable faced great challenges throughout his entire career, from the death of his biological mother to the death of wife Carol Lombard in 1942. As with any famous actor, he was the recipient of great fortune, yet it is important to recognize that his many opportunities did not preclude him from experiencing great pain and tragedy.

Rhett & Scarlett examines the life and career of one of Hollywood's most iconic leading men. Along with pictures of important people, places, and events, you will learn about Clark Gable like never before, in no time at all.

Vivien Leigh in the trailer for *Waterloo* (1940)

Vivien Leigh (1913-1967)

"I'm not a film star, I am an actress. Being a film star is such a false life, lived for fake values and for publicity." – Vivien Leigh

One of the most remarkable aspects of *Gone With the Wind* is that the quintessential Southern belle was played by Vivien Leigh, a British actress still relatively unknown in Hollywood. Vivien was an accomplished stage actress and had already appeared in foreign films during the 1930s, but she was a complete dark horse to get the iconic role she's still associated with, and it only came about because of her persistence in getting cast for the role. 30 years after *Gone With the Wind* was released, one film critic credited Selznick's "inspired casting" of Vivien Leigh as Scarlett with the film's success. Another 30 years later, the same critic wrote that Leigh "still lives in our minds and memories as a dynamic force rather than as a static presence."

While *Gone With the Wind* made Leigh a big name practically overnight, she continued to buck the usual trend by doing Broadway and even appearing on stage in London during the 1940s, instead of focusing on movies. A lot of this was no doubt due to her famous marriage to Laurence Olivier, himself an accomplished stage and film actor. At the same time, Vivien became notorious for being difficult to work with and unusually temperamental, a byproduct of bipolar disorder that frequently affected her mood and occasionally left her incoherently hysterical.

Nevertheless, Vivien was able to recapture the magic in 1951's *A Streetcar Named Desire*, which cast her in the role of Southern belle yet again. Phyllis Harnoll praised Leigh's Blanche DuBois by saying that, in the London stage production of the play, she showed, "proof of greater powers as an actress than she had hitherto shown". In fact, it was actually during her time as DuBois that she reached the pinnacle of her stage career. Likewise, her role in the movie was described as one "of the greatest performances ever put on film" and "one of those rare performances that can truly be said to evoke both fear and pity."

Unfortunately, her life and career faced constant upheaval by both her mental and physical maladies, including tuberculosis, which led to a premature death in 1967. *Rhett & Scarlett* examines the life and career of one of Hollywood's most famous actresses. Along with pictures of important people, places, and events, you will learn about Vivien Leigh like never before, in no time at all.

Chapter 1: William Clark Gable

"I eat and sleep and go to the bathroom just like anyone else. I'm just a lucky slob from Ohio who happened to be in the right place at the right time." – Clark Gable

William Clark Gable was born on February 1, 1901, the first child of William Henry "Will" Gable and Adeline Hershelman. He was born in the same small Midwestern town where Adeline had been born and raised, and he grew up an only child for the duration of his upbringing. Although his first name is mostly forgotten today, he was named after his father, and Clark was actually his middle name. Will and Adeline had great difficulty deciding on the name for their son; Adeline preferred "Clark," yet her husband intended to name his son after himself. Ironically, the father of a man Life magazine once called "all man and then some" felt that the name Clark was not masculine enough, an opinion that actually reflected his own insecure masculinity and the way in which that shortcoming affected how he would raise his son. In the end, the compromise was that Clark would be named after his father but identified as Clark for most of his life.

While the name issue was a relatively trivial matter, the argument concerning Clark's name was indicative of the unharmonious marriage between Will and Adeline. From the time of their marriage onward, Will's commitment toward his wife was less than complete, as he spent much of his time out of the house. Even though much of his time was accounted for while working in the oil fields, he paid scant attention to the wishes of his wife, and the saga concerning the naming of their son reflects the manner in which Will was unsympathetic to the best wishes of his wife. The personality clash between Clark's parents is largely attributable to personal backgrounds, and it's easy to see why their marriage would be unsuccessful even from the start. There was a clear religious divide between the two, as William was a devout Methodist but Adeline was Catholic; one of the few times Adeline's preferences was honored occurred when Clark was baptized, despite the fact that William had no desire to have the service performed. In light of the significant religious divide separating them, one could reasonably question why Will and Adeline were married to begin with, and the most likely explanation is simply that it was a marriage of convenience. By the time of their marriage, they were each approaching 30; which was especially confining for Adeline, who had already reached the age in which people of the era considered old for a single woman. Will had his own pressure to raise and support a family, since he had acquired a reputation for gambling and chasing women. During this period, Will had worked as an oil prospector, a trade that was less than reputable (widely seen as a fool's errand), and Adeline's parents could not have been confident that their son-in-law would adequately provide for their daughter. As a result, it was not difficult to predict that the marriage would be rife with acrimony, but there were clear motives for both of Clark's parents.

Will was well aware of the fact that Adeline's parents were not fond of him, and he grew paranoid that her parents would intervene and attempt to break up the marriage (Bret). For this reason, he and his new wife moved to Cadiz, Ohio shortly after the marriage, where he found more steady employment working in an oil field. This career shift was largely borne out of necessity; the oil boom had long come and gone, and there was simply no way of supporting a family without steady employment. However, even after finding a more reputable job, Will continued to treat his wife with a complete lack of respect, spending the vast majority of his time outside of the house and continuing to sleep with other women (Bret).

Complicating the marriage was that Adeline began suffering from severe health ailments even before Clark was born. Given that medical knowledge was relatively rudimentary at the beginning of the 20th century, it is difficult to pinpoint exactly what her afflictions were, but it is believed that she suffered from a heart condition and may also have experienced epileptic seizures (Bret). In any event, her health took an extreme turn for the worse during the spring of 1900, around the time that she became pregnant with Clark. Her health complications nearly prevented Clark from ever having been born; had Adeline opted to have surgery, she would have needed to abort her child. The decision to keep Clark amounted to a form of martyrdom, a belief that her child's fate would prove better than her own. It was clear that she would not live to raise her baby, and she passed away just six months after Clark's birth in February of 1901. The official cause of death was listed as epilepsy, although she may have died due to a brain tumor.

After his wife's death, Will made the unceremonious decision to erase many of his son's ties to his deceased mother. First, the birth certificate was revised to state that Clark had been born in Cadiz. Not only was this factually incorrect, but the fact that Hopedale was the town in which Adeline's family still resided implicitly declared that Will wanted nothing to do with his in-laws. In addition, Will refused to provide his son with a proper Catholic upbringing, sparking outrage from Adeline's family. Clark was nearly cut off entirely from his mother's extended family, yet a truce was established when it was agreed that Clark could spend time with Adeline's brother Charles.

It is unlikely that Adeline's death left Will terribly distraught, and there is a strong probability that they would have eventually opted for a divorce had Adeline lived longer. However, her death left Will in the precarious position of being tasked with raising and providing for his own son. Fully cognizant that he had no relatives who could perform this task, when Clark was two years of age, Will arranged for Clark to live with Adeline's brother Charles and his wife, who lived in rural Pennsylvania. Although he would be too young to remember his experience living with his aunt and uncle, they provided him with stability that had been absent for the previous year-and-a-half of his life.

While Clark was living with his aunt and uncle, Will began dating once again and soon found a new spouse. His second wife, Jennie Dunlap, was the daughter of a coal miner and worked as a seamstress. Given that she lived in the same boarding lodge in Cadiz where Will worked, it was easy for the relationship to progress swiftly, and they married on April 16, 1903, less than two years after Adeline's death. Jennie was Will's age and, like Adeline, had already reached the point at which she was identified as an "old maid." Whether or not her decision to marry Will was a desperate move is unclear, but to her credit, she was entirely willing to assist in raising Clark. In fact, she and Will would not have any children together themselves, so Clark continued to be an only child.

Immediately after marrying Jennie, Will purchased a four-acre property in Hopedale, Ohio, and he took Clark back from Charles. After two years separated from his father, Clark was united once again with Will, but the family situation remained far from perfect. As with his first marriage, there was a sizeable personality difference between Will and his wife; while Will projected an image of hyper-masculinity, Jennie was more artistically inclined, and Clark inherited his own love for art from his stepmother. She taught Clark the piano, and Clark took music lessons. Although Will did not approve of art or literature, he did not forcefully prevent his son from reading or pursuing his own interests. Clark displayed a talent for music, and at the age of 13 he became the only boy in the local men's band.

Naturally, a boy who grew up and became known for his virility was also an athlete. During his youth, Clark had already developed a strong physique, and he played several sports, including swimming, baseball, and track. Not surprisingly, Will approved of the sports. Nevertheless, despite reaching his adult height by the age of 13, Gable was ridiculed throughout his childhood for being gentle and having a high-pitched voice that undermined his rugged physique. He was also meticulously well-groomed, a trait that was instilled in him by his stepmother. Growing up in decidedly non-cosmopolitan rural Ohio, Gable qualified as something of a dandy.

Clark as a young boy

Clark as a teenager

Even as a teenager, Clark bore fundamental similarities and differences to the man he would later become. First, he retained the sturdy frame he possessed as a youth, and it would be years before his body began to go soft. Many of Gable's film performances showcase the athletic virtues he displayed as a teenager, particularly his early 1930s movies. At the same time, one of the fundamental aspects of Gable's star image is that the dandy in him never entirely went away; Christopher Spicer described his attention to detail as an adult:

> "Clark Gable didn't only look clean, he *was* clean. He showered several times a day, never using a tub because he couldn't bear to sit in dirty water. He shaved his chest and under his arms, and his bed linen was changed every day. He was

invariably impeccably dressed in public. His suits and jackets were handmade for him at Dick Caroll's in Beverley Hills and at Brooks Brothers in New York, from where he would order them ten at a time. They were all arranged in his wardrobes by color and size and tagged with the purchase date." (3).

It's immediately clear that Gable was an aesthete of the highest order, but this would not be enough to raise him to the level of the Hollywood elite. Rather, Gable's genius as an actor lay in his ability to combine the rugged masculinity required of a Hollywood leading man with the soft, immaculately-groomed aura of a sophisticated gentleman. While it would be years before Gable would project the assuredness he would display on screen, it is important to recognize that the foundation for his later persona was established even as a teenager. It also explains why Gable once claimed, "I'm no actor and I never have been. What people see on the screen is me."

Unfortunately for Gable, as a teenager he was an aesthete living in a region of the country that expected its men to find employment as manual laborers. Most children in Hopedale ended their schooling altogether after graduating from the 8th grade, after which they worked alongside their fathers. Clark was never an especially committed student, but manual labor wasn't for him either, so he entered Hopedale High School in September 1915. The enrollment for the entire school numbered just 28, with eight in Clark's grade. There were three teaches, one of whom also served as superintendent and another who assumed the responsibilities of the principal (Spicer). Even though Gable didn't care much for studying, high school did serve the productive end of exposing him to acting, and he appeared in school productions. However, during his time at Hopedale High School, several of Clark's best friends left town, devastating him and leaving Clark with little motivation to further his education.

Clark's teenage years were further complicated by a catastrophic business decision made by his father. By the time Clark reached high school, Will had become moderately successful financially, leading him to invest in oil drilling. But when it was discovered that the hole was dry, Will lost a great deal of money, forcing the family to sell their property in the late summer of 1917 (Spicer). Shortly thereafter, they purchased a 74-acre farm near Ravenna, Ohio, a rural town just outside Akron. The town was just 60 miles away from Hopedale, yet Clark struggled with moving to an insular community (not unlike Hopedale) where he had no connections. Upon arriving, he enrolled in Edinburgh Centralized High School, another tiny institution, where he was one of just 24 students (Spicer). His experience there was miserable from the start, and Clark dropped out of school permanently in November of 1917.

Once he was finished with school, Gable had no employment prospects outside of working on his father's farm, and though he worked for his father for a brief while in 1917, he found the work disagreeable. Speaking of the experience years later, he noted that he was simply not cut out to be a farmer: "I fed the hogs and the rest of the stock, plowed in the spring till every muscle ached, forked hay in the hot sun until I was sweating an impressive mop of calluses. I did what I was expected to do on the farm, but it takes a certain knack for farming in the old-fashioned way. I just didn't have what it takes." (Spicer 21).

Not surprisingly, Clark's time on the farm proved short-lived, and Jennie encouraged him to seek employment outside of the farm. He subsequently worked as a water-carrier at one of the local mines, a menial job that paid $5 per day, but by early winter, he had saved enough money to purchase his father's car. After that, Clark and a group of friends left rural Ohio for Akron, which was experiencing rapid industrialization at the time. Clark did not move to Akron with employment prospects lined up; the move was very much a last resort motivated by the fact that he simply could not continue working for his father. Eventually, he was able to find work as a clerk for the Miller Rubber Company, earning $100 per month, less than he had made at the mine. Still, the meager sum was enough for Clark to rent a room, and he quickly absorbed himself in the city life.

Although they were not located far apart, the difference between Clark's previous hometowns and Akron cannot be overstated and. For the first time, Clark was exposed to plays and films, and after viewing a stage production of *Bird of Paradise*, Clark made it his goal to become an actor. In efforts to meet people in the business and ingratiate himself, Gable developed an obeisant attitude toward the local actors, essentially becoming an errand-boy for them. Clark was willing to perform any role so long as it would bring him closer to the performers, and even though he was unable to find acting opportunities himself, Clark's time in Akron was instrumental in nurturing his desire to eventually become a professional actor.

It is impossible to determine whether Clark would have been able to eventually become an actor while living in Akron. Late in 1919, Jennie fell ill and passed away early in 1920, and after he became a widower yet again, Will moved to Tulsa, Oklahoma, where he worked at an oilfield. Unfortunately for the young man, even though Jennie's will stipulated that Clark was to receive $300, he was denied access to the money until he turned 21. Clark was exceptionally close to his stepmother, and it has even been alleged that many of his future relationships were attempts to reconstruct the dynamic he had with her (Bret). He was only 18, but he had already endured the death of his mother and then his stepmother. Finding himself in a vulnerable moment, Clark agreed to join his father in Tulsa.

While many Hollywood stars start off with good fortune, Clark Gable's childhood was filled with family tragedy and feelings of displacement. Given his love for acting and music, it is entirely possible that he would have thrived had he been born in a more urban setting, but he was relegated to outsider status in rural Ohio. It would be several years before he would be able to project the confidence he exuded in his films, but even after reaching Hollywood, he still possessed a melancholic undercurrent stemming from his upbringing. As an adult, Gable was quick to deflect attention from his childhood, and his acting career was very much an escape from an imprisoning landscape. Paradoxically, Clark's youth was quite transitory and saw him shift locations on a number of occasions, yet his early years were at the same time quite static, as he was forced to live in small towns with few outlets for his artistic interests. Ultimately, he would be unable to find any professional satisfaction until he reached his 20s.

Chapter 2: Vivian Hartley

Vivien Leigh, the English actress who would make her career playing two "belles" from the American South, was born in neither England nor the United States. She was born near a plantation, but one that manufactured tea, not cotton. Vivian Mary Hartley was born in Darjeeling, India on November 5, 1913, and for a woman whose romantic adventures would one day fascinate the world, she must have had more than one laugh about the fact that she was born on the campus of an all-boys boarding school: St. Paul's School in Darjeeling. Her parents had come to the school that summer to escape the heat of their home in Ootacamund, India, where Vivian's father, Ernest Hartley, was stationed. Hartley was a stockbroker serving as an officer in England's Indian Calvary during the last days of the British Empire. The English considered themselves rulers in India, and Hartley, along with his wife, Gertrude Mary France, lived like royalty.

It was from her mother that Vivian got her dark, mysterious looks. Gertrude always claimed to be Irish, but records seem to indicate that one of Vivian's parents (probably her mother) was actually Indian, which would certainly explain Vivian's dark hair and tip-tilted eyes. However, when she married Ernest in London in 1912, Gertrude knew that the prejudices of the time would necessitate her keeping her heritage a secret, at least for a time. There is another possible reason for Vivian's arresting looks, one also attributed to her mother. Gertrude told friends that she spent part of every day of her pregnancy staring at the beautiful Himalayan mountains, and she believed, perhaps because of legend or maybe maternal instinct, that meditating on such beauty would make her child beautiful. Whatever the reason, in Vivian's case, it worked.

Gertrude and Vivian

Regardless of the reasons for Vivian's physical qualities, the Hartley's doted on their baby girl and were determined to give her all the advantages life could hold, the first of which was a devoted Indian nanny who would accompany them back to Ootacamund from Darjeeling. Once home, the infant girl was set up in a nursery that would rival any in Britain, where she was fed and bathed and aired. In fact, given her serene surroundings and the love of both parents, she would later apologize to the press for not having a more interesting childhood: "I'm sorry it isn't a better Cinderella-story. I wasn't a poor girl, and didn't even have the common-place experience of being opposed by stern parents. Father was a stock broker in India, and I was born there. When I began longing to go on the stage, he and mother gave me every opportunity. Sent me to dramatic school in Paris, to Bavaria, and to London's Royal Academy of Dramatic Art."

Of course, all that was still years in the future when little Vivian played in the cool shade out of the Indian sun. In 1917, Ernest was sent to Bangalore to train horses for British troops fighting in World War I, and he was so concerned about the dangers of traveling with his wife and child during wartime that he left Gertrude and Vivian back in Ootacamund. Thus, it was there Vivian made her stage debut at the age of 3, reciting the woeful tale of "Little Bo Peep." The audience, made up of her mother's amateur theatre group and some other friends, found her performance enchanting; one woman later referred to her as "a bewitching little girl."

Alone in a foreign country, Gertrude devoted herself to introducing her daughter to all things English. The mother and daughter could regularly be found curled up on a couch reading Hans Christian Anderson's fairy tales and Lewis Carroll's story of Alice and her adventures on the other side of the looking glass. Naturally, there was nothing that captured the little girl's imagination quite like the tales of Rudyard Kipling, with so many of them set in the land where she lived. At the same time, Gertrude always planned to send her daughter home to England as soon as she was old enough to start school. Gertrude was a devout Catholic and wanted a strict convent-run education for her daughter, but initially it seemed that the war might prevent the two from travelling home. Thankfully, the conflict ended just in time for 6 year old Vivian to be enrolled as a boarding school girl at the Convent of the Sacred Heart in Southwest London. It may strike modern parents as odd that such devoted parents would send such a young child away to school, especially since two years would pass before they could travel home again to see her, but that was the practice among the upper classes in England in the years before World War II.

As the youngest child in school Vivian was, according to one fellow pupil, "cossetted and pampered by the nuns." This may have been the case for any of several reasons. For one thing, she was obviously "the baby of the family", and she was also further away from her mother and father than the other girls were. Other girls were able to go home for the holidays, but Vivian had to remain at school with the sisters who felt so sorry for their little charge that they allowed her to keep a kitten and let it sleep with her. Perhaps the biggest reason why the others doted on Vivian was her own good looks; even as a child her beauty smoothed her way through life. Lady Patricia Quinn, who attended Sacred Heart with Vivian, later recalled, "I can see her now --- so tiny and delicately made, with wonderful large blue eyes ad chestnut wavy hair nearly to her waist --- the tiny retroussé nose, and the only complexion I have ever seen that really was like a peach."

Young Vivian

Thanks to the treatment, and maybe because she was so young, Vivian adjusted quickly to convent life, despite the fact the seeds of her bipolar condition were already present. She found the quiet and order of life comforting, and if anything, the discipline that she learned in her early days may have helped her better control her emotions later in life. And even though the Sisters were certainly not trying to produce Hollywood starlets, they nonetheless succeeded in giving the world at least two great actresses. Vivian attended Sacred Heart with a wild Irish redhead two years older than herself named Maureen O'Sullivan, who later recalled that little Vivian often spoke of her determination to be "a great actress" someday. Vivian herself explained, "When I come into the theatre I get a sense of security. I love an audience. I love people, and I act because I like trying to give pleasure to people."

Maureen O'Sullivan

Maureen O'Sullivan was not the only friend Vivian made in school. She seemed to really care about her classmates, which made her popular among them, and she especially enjoyed surprising her peers with gifts, another habit she would maintain throughout her life. Since Vivian's parents were wealthy and she was their only child, it was easy for her to come up with tokens both big and small for the other girls at school. Her birthplace in India made her exotic, and her desire to please made her attractive, a combination that few in her life could ever resist. However, while Vivian might easily have won prizes for her popularity, none were forthcoming for her academic prowess because she was an average student who preferred to turn her attentions toward the arts rather than traditional subjects. She took every performing arts class offered and tried out for roles in all the school's plays, often getting the part she wanted or at least one nearly as good. After debuting as the Mustarseed, a fairy in *A Midsummer Night's Dream*, she went on to play Miranda in *The Tempest*. Sadly for the aspiring young actress, she did not do very well in these roles, to the extent that her high-pitched voice and failure to properly memorize her lines once drove the girl producing a play to hit her on the head with a candlestick.

In 1927, the Hartleys decided that it was time for 13 year old Vivian to leave the convent school and see more of the world, so they withdrew her from Sacred Heart and took her abroad to complete her education. In this, as in so many other areas of her life, the Hartleys were determined to give Vivian the best. She did not attend just one finishing school but several, including studying French in Paris, all the while making frequent trips with her French tutor to the best theatres in the City of Lights. Then it was on to Bavaria, where she mastered German and soaked up all the culture that Vienna and Salzburg had to offer. For the rest of her life, Vivian praised the value of her education: "Apart from the fact that I learnt to speak several languages more or less fluently, and had an opportunity of studying diction and the theatre in many countries, I met people of all types and nationalities. They gave me that flexibility of mind which is so necessary to an artist, and taught me, I hope, understanding. Through knowing them I have always been able to recognize the characters I play, and love them."

Ironically, Vivian's time in Germany shaped her in a way never intended by her parents. She was a young lady of good family whose parents had enrolled her in a good finishing school, but as she would later recall, "That meant that, being a girl, I had to learn What Every Hausfrau should know, and I hated it. That was one of the things that helped me make up my mind to become an actress." She became even more determined to go on stage when she returned to London and saw her old friend Maureen O'Sullivan in a film playing in the West End of London. Thankfully, the Hartleys were just as supportive of Vivian's plans to become an actress as any parents of that era could be. When she finished up her European tour, Vivian, now 18, gained admission to the Royal Academy of Dramatic Art in London, and although her instructors later spoke well of her once she was a star, Vivian would later remember that she did not do as well as she would have liked at the academy: "In fact, all my reports from the academy were very bad. I did a play called Caesar's Wife, by Somerset Maugham, and I remember the report saying, 'Why are you so bad? Is it because you have too much sense of humor?' Well I don't know what the reason was, but I was very shocking. I expect I didn't concentrate."

Her troubles concentrating may have been due to something else entirely. By the end of 1931, the aspiring actress had fallen in love.

Chapter 3: Starting Careers

Clark as a young man

"Every picture I make, every experience of my private life, every lesson I learn are the keys to my future. And I have faith in it." – Clark Gable

After the death of Clark's stepmother, Will encouraged his son to join him in Tulsa, promising Clark that he would find acting opportunities should he relocate. Clark agreed and arrived in Tulsa in 1920, where he joined his father in the oilfields (Bret). It is not entirely clear why Will asked his son to move; he may have grown tired of being estranged from his son, but he had never shown any great commitment to Clark, so it's hard to understand why Will would express interest in seeing his son after Clark had reached adulthood. An even more difficult decision to rationalize is why exactly Clark acquiesced in joining his father in Oklahoma; Will promised acting opportunities, but there is little reason why Clark should have trusted his father, who had never shown any regard for his personal interests. Moreover, Will had always frowned upon Clark's interest in the arts and would surely have scoffed at the notion of his son actually becoming an actor. It was ultimately an act of trickery that brought Clark to Oklahoma, where there were no acting jobs to be found, and Clark was trapped into working as a manual laborer.

Life in the oilfields was only marginally better for Clark than working on his father's farm. The pack-like mentality of the oil workers forced Gable to subdue the gentler aspects of his personality, and he adopted the rowdy lifestyle that was par for the course for the oil men. He began drinking heavily and picking up prostitutes, and it should be noted that a love for women and alcohol were aspects of Gable's personality that never went away, even after the public spotlight was cast upon him in Hollywood. He later admitted to liking brothels, saying of them, "When it's over it's over. No questions, no tears, no farewell kisses." He also talked at length about his love of women, noting, "Types really don't matter. I have been accused of preferring blondes. But I have known some mighty attractive redheads, brunettes, and yes, women with grey hair. Age, height, weight haven't anything to do with glamour… I am intrigued by glamorous women…A vain woman is continually taking out a compact to repair her makeup. A glamorous woman knows she doesn't need to."

Of course, the reckless attitude Gable assumed while living in Oklahoma is not only attributable to the standards set by his peers but can also easily be read as an expression of alienation. He was trapped in a job he had no enthusiasm for, and he was unable to access the inheritance money bequeathed to him by his stepmother until he turned 21. There was, therefore, very little that Gable could do to remedy his situation from 1920 through early 1922, and he toiled away alongside his father.

Naturally, Clark leapt at the chance to relocate after receiving his inheritance. In February 1922, immediately after his 21st birthday, Gable quit his job in Tulsa and left for Meadville, Pennsylvania, where he collected his money. He also started going by the name Billy, and he took up jobs that made him travel around the country. First, he left Meadville for Kansas City, where he worked for a traveling tent show assisting with the set design (Bret). This job was not dissimilar to his earlier stints as a helper to the acting troupe in Akron, and it once again brought him in close proximity to actors. The major difference was that his position with the Kansas City troupe enabled him to travel with the company, and he traveled outside of the region. When the group experienced hardship and their act was terminated in Montana, Clark and the group's pianist left for Bend, Oregon, where his friend's family resided. The exact job that Clark found in Oregon is unclear; it is believed that he either worked as a necktie salesman or as someone tasked with unloading shipments from the loading deck (Bret). Whichever job he held, Clark's first job in Oregon was a clear step up from his experience in Tulsa, but not as personally preferable to his time with the acting troupe.

Eventually, Clark found an acting opportunity with the Astoria Players, a local stock company, where he worked in the familiar position of helping with the set design. At this point, he had shown great difficulty in advancing beyond this necessary but decidedly unglamorous position, and it was only after one of the actors left the company that Gable actually received an opportunity to act. The company was not terribly successful, but Gable benefitted from the practice, since he was entirely untrained and still possessed an unusually high-pitched voice.

Gable lasted less than one year with the company, which collapsed at the start of 1923. Immediately thereafter, he returned to Oregon, where he worked for *The Oregonian* as a deliveryman and assistant in the newspaper office (Bret).

During his spare time, Gable continued to hone his skills, and in June 1923, he caught his biggest break yet when he met Josephine Dillon, an actress of moderate fame who was in town scouting actors for her own drama troupe. After auditioning, he was accepted and was finally in a position where he could receive acting instruction from someone with a substantial degree of success within the industry. For this reason, 1923 stands as one of the most significant years of Gable's entire career, and the year in which he truly solidified acting as his career.

Josephine Dillon

Thanks to Dillon's tutelage, Gable improved his many deficiencies as an actor. First, he improved his posture and learned how to comport himself with greater poise. In 1923, Gable was also underweight (possibly as a result of hepatitis, although this is not entirely substantiated), and Dillon assisted him in building his body up to the point that he could find roles as a leading man. Finally, she improved his elocution and helped train him to lower his voice. The tutelage he received from Dillon was not especially dissimilar to the formal training that most actors go through. The American public may be largely unaware of the tremendous work that goes into constructing an actor's appearance, but before Gable could attempt to make a name for himself in Hollywood, he had to first succeed in making himself fit for the gaze of the camera.

After guiding him through the technical aspects of being an actor, Dillon used her connections to secure acting opportunities. First, she secured a position for Clark in the Forest Taylor Stock

Company, which was based in Portland and enabled Clark to gain consistent acting experience. In June 1923, Gable and Dillon arrived in Hollywood, and they were married the following year. Of the five wives Gable would marry over the course of his life, his marriage to Dillon is surely the most difficult to explain. She had long been rumored to be a lesbian, and she was 17 years older than Clark. (Bret). The most probable rationale is that Gable married her out of the belief that doing so would make Dillon more likely to continue helping him further his career.

However, immediately after arriving in Hollywood, Gable had no success finding acting opportunities. He even worked in an auto garage for awhile, as he had always been a skilled mechanic, but later in 1923, he was able to find a small role in a film, thanks to a connection of Dillon's. That same year, he also made the decision to go by the name Clark again, and he also added two years to his age, holding himself out as a 24 year old. These steps completed his makeover, fully preparing him for his illustrious Hollywood career.

As with most actors, Clark Gable was unable to find significant acting parts in his first films and instead appeared as an extra. The lone exception was actually his first film, *White Man*, in which he had a very small role. He was able to find consistent acting opportunities, including two films released in 1924 and 10 the following year. Even though his acting performances were quite minor, he was also able to earn a decent living; in his first film, *White Man*, he earned $150 per week. The films in which he was cast as an extra paid considerably less (roughly $15 per day), but he was hardly a starving actor, especially with Dillon supporting him.

Many of his earliest films were actually quite significant on their own, even though he did not have major roles. For example, Gable's second film, *Forbidden Paradise* (1924), was directed by the legendary Ernst Lubitsch. In fact, Clark's first major acting opportunity was to have been in Erich von Stroheim's *The Merry Widow* (1925), but he clashed with the famous director and was relegated to once again appearing as an extra. For the first two years of his career, Gable stayed very busy but could not find his first big break. Throughout the decade, he was unable to progress through the Hollywood ranks, but his situation was far less dire than it might appear. He had the luxury of being able to depend on Dillon, who spoiled him and subsidized him quite generously.

Furthermore, when it became clear that Clark would have difficulty finding any major opportunities from the outset, he simply turned his attention to the theater. As the 1920s progressed, he began receiving increasingly more prominent acting opportunities, bringing him outside of California. In 1927 and 1928, he accepted a position with the Laskin Brothers Stock Company in Houston. After this stint was completed, he moved to New York City with Dillon and acted on Broadway.

Gable was successful in the theater and had every reason to believe that he would have a successful career as a Broadway actor, but by the end of the decade the theater began to suffer for several reasons. First, the arrival of synchronized sound in the movies made the cinema considerably more popular than the stage, as audiences were captivated by the prospect of watching singing and dialogue onscreen. But even more importantly, the Great Depression compromised the success of the theater, and actors were unable to continue finding acting opportunities. Thus, after several years acting in plays, Gable once again turned his attention back to Hollywood, moving back to California in 1930. That same year, he and Dillon divorced, putting an end to a strange marriage.

The timing makes it seem as though once he had a contract with MGM, Gable no longer relied on Dillon to advance his career and therefore found it possible to cut all ties with her, but Gable also had another pressing reason to divorce his first wife. At the time, he was involved in an affair with another woman, a Texas socialite named Marian Franklin Prentiss Lucas Langham, who went by "Ria." Clark and Ria were married in the immediate aftermath of his divorce, and they settled into Hollywood together. Unlike Dillon, Langham was firmly entrenched in the upper class, and her financial assistance had actually helped Clark with his theater career during the 1920s. As a theater patron, she and Gable met through the stage. As with his first marriage, Clark would continue to sleep with myriad women, but what his marriage lacked in fidelity it made up for in duration. He and Ria remained married for most of the decade before divorcing in 1939. Although Langham and Dillon were vastly different in their backgrounds, one similarity was that they were each far older than Clark. Langham was 47 at the time of their marriage, a substantial age discrepancy that lends credence to the belief that many of Gable's wives were surrogates for his deceased mother or stepmother.

Ria

Fortunately for Clark, his success on Broadway enabled him to find more appealing acting roles than he had found during his first stint in Hollywood. In 1930, he signed a contract with MGM that allowed him to no longer have to act as an extra. His first film upon returning was *The Painted Desert* (1931), which cast him as a brazen former criminal. As the role would suggest, Gable's niche early in his career was as a criminal, a far cry from the genteel performances he would later give. During the 1930s, gangster and crime films were exceedingly popular, and Gable proved to be successful playing men of ill repute. Clark's first headlining role was in the 1931 film *Sporting Blood*, in which he starred as a gambler who succeeds at the horse races and successfully evades the police, but he was able to reveal a broader acting talent with *Possessed* (1932), which paired him with Joan Crawford. In the film, Gable stars as a lawyer who has an affair with Crawford and in the process helps her progress through the societal ranks. The film focuses most heavily on Crawford's character, yet Gable benefitted from being able to portray a romantic dimension that had not been part of his earlier, more physical performances. Crawford later said Gable " was a king wherever he went. He walked like one, he behaved like one, and he was the most masculine man that I have ever met in my life."

Gable and Crawford in *Dance, Fools, Dance*

Two other significant films for Clark during 1932 were *Red Dust* (1932) and *No Man of Her Own* (1932). *No Man of Her Own* is notable for being the first (and only) film in which Gable appeared alongside Carole Lombard, who would later become his wife. Meanwhile, in *Red Dust*, Gable was paired with Jean Harlow, the first of six films he would appear in with her. Directed by Victor Fleming, *Red Dust* features an action-packed plot set in French Indochina, and the action plot and romantic plot converge as Jean Harlow's character becomes Gable's love interest and nurse. The film showed that Gable was capable of combining his skills as a physical actor with romantic comedy, an achievement that cannot be underestimated. Indeed, the ability to succeed in both realms at the same time meant the difference between being a B-actor and being a major star.

Gable and Jean Harlow in *Red Dust*

Meanwhile, as one acting career was beginning in earnest, another one seemed like it was about to end. In 1931, Vivian met her future husband, Herbert Leigh Holman, at the South Devon Hunt Ball, and though she may not have been looking for a husband at this particular juncture in her life, such events were popular with young people of her "set" and were designed to encourage pairings up between men and women considered suitable for each other. Holman was certainly suitable; although he was 13 years older than his future wife at the age of 31, he was nonetheless a Barrister with an established career and all that would be needed to care for a wife and family. He also came from a good family, one further up the social ladder than the Hartleys. They were married just over a year after meeting in December of 1932.

Vivian and Herbert Leigh Holman

Just like Scarlett O'Hara, Vivian became a mother shortly after becoming a wife, with her only child, Suzanne, being born on October 12, 1933. Since pregnancy was still taboo on stage, it eventually put an end to her acting plans, which may have disappointed her but pleased her husband to no end. He did not consider acting a suitable occupation for his wife, and he was only too pleased to see her settle down to her "proper" role as a wife and mother. He was soon disappointed, however, when it became clear that Vivian had other plans. She would later lament, "I was under nineteen when I married, and not quite twenty when my daughter was born. I felt too young to be the mother of a child, and very lacking in the qualities of restfulness and serenity which a mother should have. How many times since then Scarlett O'Hara's lines, speaking of her mother, have sprung to my mind: 'I always wanted to be like her, calm and kind. I certainly have turned out disappointingly.'"

Vivian and Suzanne

In the 1930s, many women did not believe that they could have it all, and while most chose motherhood over a career, those who chose to pursue a career at the expense of their family lives seem not to have suffered those bouts of guilt that so many modern women struggle with. This is perhaps because anyone wealthy enough to choose to have a career was also wealthy enough to hire a nanny, which itself was a status symbol at the time. In fact, such women had often been raised by nannies and in boarding schools themselves, and thus they suffered even less angst about such a decision. This was certainly true of Vivian, who later explained:

> "I was not cast in the mold of serenity and in my case, although you may succeed in being kind at twenty you cannot be calm, with all your life still before you, and your ambitions unfulfilled. I loved my baby as every mother does, but with the clear-cut sincerity of youth I realized that I could not abandon all though of a career on the stage. Some force within myself would not be denied expression. I took the problem to my husband and asked his advice. He was many years older that I was, a deeply kind and wise man, with the rare quality of imagination that implied tolerance and unselfishness. We decided that I should continue my studied at the Royal Academy of Dramatic Art. We took a tiny house in Little Stanhope Street and got a good nanny for the baby."

While studying at the Royal Academy, Vivien won a small part in the movie *Things Are Looking Up*, after which her agent, John Gliddon, advised her to take a stage name. Gliddon believed "Vivian Holman" was too plain for an actress, and he also rejected Vivian's first suggestion, "April Morn," but he agreed when she suggested she replace her married name with her husband's middle name. Thus was born Vivien (with an "e," not an "a") Leigh.

Leigh did well in her first film, leading Gliddon to snare her a part in a play, *The Mask of Virtue*, in 1935. Leigh would later recall fondly, "It was a romantic first night. I had a part that was both good and decorative, and I was helped by the entire cast, with that wonderful loyalty and generosity of the theatre world towards a newcomer. The fact that I was young and unknown caught the imagination of the audience. The roar of applause when the final curtain fell told me that the miracle had happened. I had arrived." Sure enough, that role would prove to be Leigh's launching pad to stardom. Her performance was praised by everyone from highly thought of theatre critics to the members of the audience. One of the things that impressed many reviewers was just how much emotion she was able to convey with her facial expressions, and also just how quickly those expressions could change. For her part, Leigh did not know exactly what to think of all the praise, as she later put it: "Some critics saw fit to be as foolish as to say that I was a great actress. And I thought, that was a foolish, wicked thing to say, because it put such an onus and such a responsibility onto me, which I simply wasn't able to carry. And it took me years to learn enough to live up to what they said for those first notices. I find it so stupid. I remember the critic very well and have never forgiven him."

Naturally, success brought with it more public attention and interviews. Always gracious, Leigh remained modestly optimistic about her future as an actress, telling one reporter, "I got my first real job only last January- in a couple of minor films. Next a part in a little theatre play, and finally this fine role in 'The Mask of Virtue.' As for plans—well, I love the real theatre and if I keep on making good after my screen contract is ended I want to appear on the stage again in London, and in Paris and Berlin." Furthermore, in the audience on opening night was Alexander Korda, a director and producer that Gliddon had tried to get to sign Leigh for his production company. Korda initially rejected, her, but after seeing her in *The Mask of Virtue*, he immediately changed her mind and offered her a film contract. This was definitely fortunate, because Leigh was unable to make herself heard once the play was moved to a larger theatre. It was obvious that her true future as an actress had to be on film.

Another man saw Vivien in *The Mask of Virtue* and was instantly intrigued by her. Laurence Olivier, already a star in his own right, went out of his way to congratulate Leigh on her performance, and he later described his first impression of her: "Apart from her looks, which were magical, she possessed beautiful poise; her neck looked almost too fragile to support her head and bore it with a sense of surprise, and something of the pride of the master juggler who can make a brilliant maneuver appear almost accidental. She also had something else: an attraction of the most perturbing nature I had ever encountered. It may have been the strangely touching spark of dignity in her that enslaved the ardent legion of her admirers." Obviously, he was soon smitten and encouraged her to audition for a role in his next film, *Fire Over England.*

Olivier and his wife, Jill Esmond, in 1930

More than any other film, *Fire Over England* changed Leigh's life by providing her with the credentials that would lead to her future stardom. In the movie, Leigh played Cynthia, a lady-in-waiting to Queen Elizabeth II, and Cynthia's major claim to fame in the movie was that she fell in love with and finally married Michael Ingolby, played by Olivier. In a classic tale of life imitating art, that is exactly what happened between the two during filming. Though each were married to other people, they embarked on a long and increasingly public affair that would eventually lead to their own marriage. At the same time, as Vivien was looking for something to read between takes, she picked up a new novel everyone was talking about: Gone With the Wind. She would later recall, "From the moment I read GWTW, I was fascinated by the lovely wayward, tempestuous Scarlett. I felt that I loved and understood her, almost as though I had known her in the flesh. When I heard that the book was to be filmed in Hollywood early in 1939 I longed to play the part…" She added, "I wanted to play Scarlett from the first time I read the book. That was in London when I was appearing in a flop play. I fell in love with the novel and I gave the rest of the cast copies of the book as opening night presents. I told them, 'If I ever go to Hollywood, it will be to play Gone With the Wind.' They all laughed and said I was crazy."

Chapter 4: Gable Tackles 1930s Hollywood

"They see me as an ordinary guy, like a construction worker or the guy who delivers your piano." – Clark Gable

In 1932 and 1933, Gable continued to find appealing acting opportunities, and altogether, he appeared in four films both years. In 1932, he noted, "I have been in show business for 12 years.

They have known me in Hollywood but two. Yet as picture-making goes, two years is a long time. Nevertheless, my advice has never been asked about a part in a picture. I found out I was going into 'Susan Lenox' in Del Monte. Read it in a paper. When I walked on the set one day, they told me I was going to play 'Red Dust' in place of John Gilbert. I have never been consulted as to what part I would like to play. I am paid not to think." But he also admitted that he tried to avoiding bad parts, stating about his acting, "I worked like a son of a bitch to learn a few tricks and I fight like a steer to avoid getting stuck with parts I can't play."

Off the movie set, Gable attracted attention for having an affair with Joan Crawford, and he quickly developed a reputation for being a womanizer. A famous story holds that Gable once looked at a publicity photograph of leading MGM actresses and remarked without hyperbole that he had slept with each of them. The inability to remain faithful stands as the greatest similarity and one of the only similarities linking him with his father. Even though Clark's endless stream of affairs positioned him in a less-than-noble light, he is a prime example of the adage that any publicity is good publicity, as his pursuits off the movie set furthered his image as one of the sexiest men in Hollywood. For his own part, Gable once said, "Hell, if I'd jumped on all the dames I'm supposed to have jumped on, I'd have had no time to go fishing."

By 1933, Clark was commanding a robust salary of $2,000 per week from MGM. For the most part, they were able to keep him busy and thereby maximize their investment in the process, but there were also periods in which they had no films available for him. As a result, MGM was eager to lend Gable to Columbia, which offered to pay him $2,500 per week to appear in *It Happened One Night* (1934). Gable had not been their first choice for the role (nor was Claudette Colbert, his costar), but Gable had shown that he could handle romantic comedy and was thus considered a serviceable replacement for Robert Montgomery, who had turned down the role. As Linda Mizejewski wrote, "In key moments of *It Happened One Night*, Gable brings to the character of Peter some of the tough-guy grittiness from his MGM image but he also shows that he is able to mock it or play against it" (103). It was, therefore, an unlikely set of circumstances that saw Gable appear in his most significant film to that point in his career.

Gable with Claudette Colbert in *It Happened One Night*

It Happened One Night was one of a number of prominent Depression-era films directed by Frank Capra, who specialized in wholesome, sentimental films that restored the promise of the American Dream. This motif resurfaces in *Mr. Deeds Goes to Town* (1936), *You Can't Take it With You* (1938), *Mr. Smith Goes to Washington* (1939), and (later) *It's a Wonderful Life* (1946). Capra's style held great appeal to the American public not only because his films suggested that everything would get better for the impoverished American viewer but because he seamlessly combined pathos with comedy in a way that was profoundly heartening for the downtrodden viewer. In *It Happened One Night* (1934), Gable stars as a newspaper reporter who has lost his job and witnesses Ellie, a wealthy socialite (played by Colbert) eloping with a man against her father's wishes. Realizing that Ellie's father has offered a reward to whoever can return his daughter to him, Gable's character threatens to cash in on his knowledge, but over the course of the film he and Colbert's character fall in love and the film concludes with their marriage.

It is not difficult to understand why *It Happened One Night* had such great appeal for the Depression-era audience. The weaving together of the reconciliation of class difference with the romantic plot allowed viewers to dream on the possibility that they might be able to meet someone who could help them overcome their unfortunate economic condition. The witty dialogue - in the proper screwball comedy tradition - also made the Gable-Colbert pairing particularly sexy, albeit in a covert way that circumvented the censorship standards of the Hays Code. For these reasons, the film stands as one of the most successful films of all time, becoming the first movie to win all five of the most decorated Academy Awards: Best Picture, Best Director, Best Screenplay, Best Actor, and Best Actress. The film could not have gone better for Gable, who not only garnered critical acclaim but also returned to MGM having proven that he could deliver an Oscar-winning performance.

After going back to MGM, Clark was once again paired with Jean Harlow, starring with her in

China Seas (1935) and *Saratoga* (1937). *China Seas* reprised the formula of casting Gable as an uber-masculine adventure hero, this time as a sea captain who reveals his romantic side as the film unfolds, eventually culminating in his union with Harlow's character. *Saratoga* was the more significant film, not only because of its more alluring plot but because of the fact that Harlow died during the production. In a freak occurrence, Harlow died of kidney failure, and the film was completed by using body doubles. Because audiences were eager to watch Harlow's final performance, *Saratoga* performed well at the box office, and it received strong reviews as well. In the film, Gable plays Duke, a racetrack bookie who eventually wins over Harlow's character, who drops her engagement with a wealthy suitor in order to be with Duke.

Gable and Harlow

The death of Jean Harlow complicated Gable's position within MGM, as the studio had suddenly lost one of its premier romantic pairings. Fortunately, Gable had acted alongside Myrna Loy on a couple of occasions, and each of his 1938 films cast him with her. The first of these, *Test Pilot* (1938), was especially successful and was nominated for an Academy Award for Best Picture. The film relied on Gable's ability to portray the action hero, and he was well-suited for the role of a fighter pilot. Like the films he appeared in with Jean Harlow, the plot involves Gable curbing his reckless instincts in the interest of the romantic plot. Gable's acting was particularly successful for the way that he combined the brashness of the action hero with the sophistication of the romantic comedy hero. As a result, in roles such as *Test Pilot*, he revealed an exceptional ability to appeal to both men and women. *Test Pilot* is an example of Gable's ability to be romantic and masculine in a 'natural' way that was simultaneously sophisticated and genuine. According to Linda Mizejewski, this naturalness formed the cornerstone of Gable's appeal: "Clark Gable's stardom in the 1930s was tied to cultural ideals and contentions about masculinity, and he went on to become one of the great masculine icons of American cinema. He became known as an actor who always 'played himself,' who expressed his rugged manliness without 'acting' on-screen, a reputation that he shared with icons John Wayne and Gary Cooper." (97).

Mizejewski recognizes how Gable (as well as John Wayne and Gary Cooper) succeeded due to his ability to provide a model for masculinity that was accessible and not tied to wealth or pretension. He was a heartthrob for women and an idol for men, and there was no actor more powerful than him by the end of the decade. He once humorously claimed, "This power that I'm supposed to have over women was never noticed when I was a stage actor on Broadway. I don't know when I got it. And by God, I can't explain it." He also talked about his popularity, asserting, "I don't believe I'm king of anything, but I know why they like to think I am. I'm not much of an actor, but I'm not bad unless it's one of those things outside my comprehension. I work hard. I'm no Adonis, and I'm as American as the telephone poles I used to climb to make a living. So men don't get sore if their women folks like me on the screen. I'm one of them, they know it, so it's a compliment to them. They see me broke, in trouble, scared of things that go bump in the night, but I come out fighting. They see me making love to Jean Harlow or Claudette Colbert and they say, 'If he can do it, I can do it,' and figure it'll be fun to go home and to make love to their wives."

As the 1930s drew to a close, Gable's marriage with Ria Langham had grown stale, and they had actually not lived together in years. Obtaining a divorce was a mere formality, and the divorce was made official in 1939, motivated in no small part by the fact that Gable had fallen in love with actress Carole Lombard. Just three months after the divorce was finalized, he and Lombard married. It is important to note that Lombard differed significantly from each of his earlier wives; where they were substantially older than him, Lombard was four years younger; unlike Dillon and Langham, one could not argue that Lombard was a substitute for his deceased stepmother. In this regard, Gable's third marriage was more adult than his earlier ones and he and Lombard were not only married but lived together as well. Gable was already 38 years of age, yet he had at last found a woman to whom he was committed.

Gable and Carole Lombard

Chapter 5: Gone With the Wind

Gable in 1938

"The public interest in my playing Rhett puzzled me. I was the only one, apparently, who didn't take it for granted that I would." – Clark Gable

"I am Scarlett O'Hara! The role is practically written for me." – Katharine Hepburn

"I know I am right for Scarlett. I can convince Mr. Selznick." - Vivien Leigh

As soon as she finished reading *Gone With the Wind*, Vivien contacted her agent and ordered him to get her a screen test for the role. There are a number of reasons why she found the role of Scarlett O'Hara so attractive. First, in the book, Scarlett, while still very young, marries a man she does not love while in love with a man she cannot have. At that point in her life, Leigh found herself in a similar situation; Holman was a good solid man and a kind husband, but she had given her heart to Olivier, a man who was married to another. Leigh may also have been attracted to a character who was not supposed to be that beautiful. In the opening lines of the book, author Margaret Mitchell wrote, "Scarlet O'Hara was not beautiful, but men seldom realized it when caught by her charm…." Leigh had often bemoaned her belief that beauty was not necessarily an asset for an actress, saying, "People think that if you look fairly reasonable, you can't possibly act, and as I only care about acting, I think beauty can be a great handicap, if you really want to look like the part you're playing, which isn't necessarily like you." Of course, this was not a problem with the character of Scarlett, who had "an arresting face, pointed of chin, square of jaw. Her eyes were pale green without a touch of hazel, starred with bristly black lashes and slightly tilted at the ends. Above them, her thick black brows slanted upward, cutting a startling oblique line in her magnolia-white skin…." Except for the eyes (Leigh's did have more than a touch of hazel), this description fit Vivien to a tee.

Vivien in the late 1930s

At the same time, there did not have to be any special reason for Leigh to want to play Scarlett. It seemed that every actress in America, and many in other parts for the world, were also dying to play the Southern belle. Leigh was determined to have the part, telling one reporter, "I've cast myself as Scarlett O'Hara." Another reporter recalled, "Somebody turned to Olivier and said, 'Larry you'd be marvelous as Rhett Butler.' He laughed it off, but the suggestion was not too preposterous…discussion of the casting went on in a desultory fashion, until the new girl, Vivien Leigh, brought it to a sudden stop. She drew herself up on the rain-swept deck, all five feet nothing of her, pulled a coat round her shoulders and stunned us with the sibylline utterance: "Larry won't play Rhett Butler, but I shall play Scarlett O'Hara. Wait and see..."

Of course, the problem was that Leigh was still a relatively new actress on the other side of the world from where *Gone With The Wind* was being filmed. In fact, when the movie's producer, David O. Selznick, received the request from her agent, his response was, "I have no enthusiasm for Vivien Leigh. Maybe I will have, but as yet have never even seen photograph of her. I will be seeing Fire Over England shortly, at which time will of course see Leigh."

Selznick

While waiting for her big chance to play Scarlett, Vivien continued to act by playing Ophelia opposite of Olivier in *Hamlet*, which was being staged by the Old Vic Theatre at Elsinore Castle in Denmark. This was a boon for Leigh because the castle's smaller space and stone walls provided excellent acoustics to carry her often too soft voice. However, it was during this time in Denmark that Olivier first noticed the mood swings brought about Leigh's bipolar disorder. According to his comments years later, just before the curtain rose, she fell into a rage and began screaming at him for no reason. As he was trying to calm her down and reason with her, she suddenly became very quiet and seemed almost to be in another world. She soon snapped out of the mood, performed well on stage, and didn't even remember what had happened the next day.

Bipolar disorder typically manifests itself in early adulthood and is made worse by stress. At this time, Vivien's stress was brought about by the close scrutiny of the press. According to one reporter writing an article about her during this era, "This tiny, slender-boned little creature with the grey eyes and delicate heart-shaped face, has more responsibilities on her shoulders than most women twice her age would care for. She is able to take them lightly and yet competently because - having had marriage and motherhood and stardom thrust on her before she was twenty - she has had to solve a problem that has wrecked the lives of women far more experienced than herself. She has learnt the trick of combining marriage with a strenuous career." In reality, the problem was that she was not successfully balancing her marriage with the rest of her life. She and Olivier were living together even as both their spouses refused to grant them divorces, and had this situation become public, their careers would have been in jeopardy because the film industry had strict rules against public adultery. Thus, she was forced to live a double life that caused her behavior to become increasingly erratic.

In 1937, Leigh returned to the big screen, starring as German spy Madeleine Goddard in *Dark Journey*, which earned her praise from audiences and led to her receiving top billing in the little-known film *Storm in a Tea Cup*. That appearance boosted her further, after which she joined an all-star cast in *A Yank at Oxford* in 1938. This film, in which she played opposite Americans Robert Taylor and Lionel Barrymore, proved to be critically important to her goal of playing Scarlett O'Hara because it was the first of her films to be seen widely in the United States. Thus, American audiences, as well as directors and producers, got a chance to see the English actress ahead of her lobbying for a part in their biggest movie ever.

Following the completion of *St. Martin's Lane* in 1938, Leigh flew to Hollywood to lobby for the part of Scarlett herself. The timing was convenient, because Olivier was there working on *Wuthering Heights*, and she longed to be near him. What she seemed to fail to realize was that the standards of behavior in Hollywood were even stricter than those in London. Therefore, while she could see her beloved lover, she had to make sure that no one ever found out how close the two actually were; America would never accept an adulteress as Scarlett O'Hara.

From the start, the legendary Selznick had great ambitions for the film, going so far as to purchase the film rights to it before the novel it was based off was released in 1936. The book became an instant classic, selling a million copies within 6 months, after which it was awarded the Pulitzer Prize in 1937 (Taylor). That Selznick had the savvy to purchase the film rights to the novel before it was even distributed to the public reflected his love for adapting literary classics, an aspect of his personality that frequently leads critics to dismiss him as a slave to the novel. Despite this, however, Molly Haskell explains that Selznick assumed a great deal of risk with the production, and the book's grand narrative represented its saving grace:

> "It's easy to poke fun at the literary, and sometimes pseudoliterary, ambitions of Selznick, yet he could have lost his reputation as well as his shirt, could have been a laughingstock...There were many good reasons (mostly financial) that so few studios were eager to bid on the book, but there was one overwhelming argument in its favor: the generalized nature of the story, the very lack of historical detail with which critics reproached it, allowed it to speak of timeless love and loss, of family and romance, of a titanic struggle against national catastrophe that reverberated with all the struggles, past and to come, in a young nation's history." (35).

Haskell's explanation alludes to the way in which, despite much of the film being set in the

Civil War era, the film still had great relevance in 1930s America, a landscape that was itself struggling with many of the same themes explored in the novel, such as economic loss and racism. In addition, broad themes such as family loss and broken romances were captivating to any audience. Selznick's interest in producing the film may have stemmed from his love for the novel, but it is clear in any case that the plot was well-suited for the screen.

For all of Selznick's literary leanings, it is also true that he was committed to transforming the text into a visual spectacle that made the film far from a mere retelling of the book. Alan David Vertrees discusses how during the production of *Gone With the Wind*, Selznick balanced his need to remain faithful to the novel with his desire to produce a great work of visual art:

> "Selznick developed the script with one eye on [Margaret] Mitchell's novel (and on the public's response to it) and the other on his visualization of the finished film. Indeed, the preliminary design of the film—not only as story but also as spectacle and cinematic achievement—was in many ways as important as the script itself. Selznick saw *Gone With the Wind* not only as an adaptation of an enormously popular novel, but also as a display of the full potential of cinematic art." (xii).

The technical accomplishments of *Gone with the Wind* are on display throughout the film, as it was one of the earliest and most successful examples of Technicolor. In addition, Selznick hired Victor Fleming (who directed *The Wizard of Oz* that same year) to direct the film and the famed Max Steiner to arrange the score. As a result, Selznick was rewarded with a film whose technical virtuosity went almost unmatched.

Leigh may have hoped that being with Olivier would help settle her moods, but by this time her behavior had become so erratic that Alexander Korda was threatening not to renew her contract. Nevertheless, she arrived in Hollywood at the height of the now legendary "Search for Scarlett." Smelling a prime publicity stunt, producer David O Selznick had staged an elaborate plot to entice as many actresses and would-be actresses to try out for the part as possible. Supposedly he was looking for an unknown to play the famed daughter of the South and debutantes rushed in from every part of Georgia, Mississippi and Alabama, but they clearly stood little chance against such women as Lucille Ball and Bette Davis, both of whom also made screen tests for the part.

What few people knew was that a 25 year old British actress had the inside track for the role of Scarlett. For one thing, Leigh's agent in America was a member of the Myron Selznick Agency, which was owned by David's brother and also represented Olivier. David had seen Leigh in *A Yank at Oxford* and thought her a good actress, albeit "too British" for the role, but when Olivier introduced Leigh to Myron Selznick, he felt he had just the woman his brother was looking for.

Myron still needed a way to get David's attention, and he found it on December 9, 1938, after

David began shooting the famous scene for the burning of Atlanta. Sauntering up to his big brother, he introduced Leigh to David with the now famous words, "Here genius, meet your Scarlett O'Hara." The next day, David wrote to his wife, "Myron rolled in just exactly too late, arriving about a minute and a half after the last building had fallen and burned and after the shorts were completed. With him were Larry Olivier and Vivien Leigh. Shhhhh: she's the Scarlett dark horse, and looks damned good. Not for anybody's ears but your own: it's narrowed down to Paulette Goddard, Jean Arthur, Joan Bennett, and Vivien Leigh. We're making final tests this week…"

Once director George Cukor saw her tests, he declared that Vivien Leigh was indeed the one, and a few days later, Selznick announced that Scarlett O'Hara would be played by an English actress most American had never heard of. Needless to say, a lot of people were stunned. One of the biggest concerns for both the professionals and the public was Leigh's accent. In one of the few interviews allowed by Selznick, she was asked about this problem and replied with grace, "As a matter of fact, we English are inclined to drop our r's and speak in a rather lackadaisical way, just as the Southerners do. But, even so, any actress worth her salt should be able to handle any accent required. I found the Southern much easier than a Scottish accent, for instance. In fact, I got it so well that several times I was told I was too Southern. And three hours of heavy Southern accents would be too much for any audience to take." Vivien wrote back to her husband, "You will never guess what has happened and no one is more surprised than me. You know that I only came out here for a week. Well just two days before I was supposed to leave, the people who are making Gone With the Wind saw me and said would I make a test - so what could I do and now I am working frantically hard and rehearsing, and studying a Southern accent which I don't find difficult anyway... The part has now become the biggest responsibility one can imagine and yet it would be absurd not to do it given the chance..."

Cukor

Sadly, getting the Southern accent right proved to be the least of Leigh's problems when filming *Gone With the Wind*. For one thing, George Cukor, whom she and Olivia de Havilland (Melanie) both loved, was fired by Selznick and replaced with Victor Fleming. While Cukor was considered by many to be a "woman's director," Fleming got along better with Clark Gable and Leslie Howard, ad he had problems making Leigh understand what he wanted in a scene, leading to more than one angry eruption on her part. To compensate, she and de Havilland began meeting secretly with Cukor outside of filming hours to get a sense of how they should portray their characters.

Leigh got along well with de Havilland better than she did Howard or Gable, but she and Gable's wife, Carol Lombard, became friends. Havilland would later defend Leigh from accusations that she had been difficult to work with on the film, writing in 2006, "Vivien was impeccably professional, impeccably disciplined on Gone with the Wind. She had two great concerns: doing her best work in an extremely difficult role and being separated from Larry [Olivier], who was in New York." Indeed, missing Olivier was a big part of her problem at this time. While she spoke with him frequently on the phone, he was on the other side of the continent and they were only able to see other occasionally."

Given the ideal match between Clark Gable and Vivien Leigh, it may come as a surprise to learn that Gable had no intention of appearing in the film. Gary Cooper had already turned down the role of Rhett Butler and allegedly claimed, "Gone With the Wind is going to be the biggest flop in Hollywood history. I'm glad it'll be Clark Gable who's falling flat on his nose, not me." It was only through Lombard's urging that Gable agreed to take on the role (Harris). Gable was also the actor that producer David O. Selznick wanted. Always careful of cultivating his image, Gable explained his reservations about taking the role: "I found myself trapped by a series of circumstances over which I had no control. It was a funny feeling. I think I know now how a fly must react after being caught in a spider's web. Scarlett doesn't always love Rhett. It's the first time that the girl isn't sure that she wants me from the minute she sets eyes on me."

As it turned out, Gable was as suave as ever playing Rhett Butler, but he admitted it was a difficult role: "I discovered that Rhett was even harder to play than I had anticipated. With so much of Scarlett preceding his entrance, Rhett's scenes were all climaxes. There was a chance to build up to Scarlett, but Rhett represented drama and action every time he appeared. He didn't figure in any of the battle scenes, being a guy who hated war, and he wasn't in the toughest of the siege of Atlanta shots. What I was fighting for was to hold my own in the first half of the picture - which is all Vivien's - because I felt that after the scene with the baby, Bonnie, Rhett could control the end of the film. That scene where Bonnie dies, and the scene where I strike Scarlett and she accidentally tumbles down stairs, thus losing her unborn child, were the two that worried me most." Olivia de Havilland explained how she had to try to get Gable to cry during one of the scenes, "Oh, he would not do it. He would not! Victor (Fleming) tried everything with him. He tried to attack him on a professional level. We had done it without him weeping several times and then we had one last try. I said, 'You can do it, I know you can do it and you will be wonderful.' Well, by heaven, just before the cameras rolled, you could see the tears come up at his eyes and he played the scene unforgettably well. He put his whole heart into it."

Of course, in the end it was all worth it. Gone With the Wind is still considered one of the greatest motion pictures of all time, and the film has been mythologized into American culture to the point that Rhett Butler's final parting line to Scarlett - "Frankly, my dear, I don't give a damn." - has become part of the American lexicon. At the same time, there is a wide gulf between the love expressed toward the film by the American public and the relative contempt toward it exuded by critics. Alan David Vertrees discussed this dynamic, writing, "What are we to do with *Gone With the Wind*? The most popular and commercially successful film of all time, embraced by popular historians and journalistic critics while generally reviled by 'serious' scholars and cinephiles, *Gone With the Wind* stands as both a monument to classical Hollywood and a monumental anomaly" (ix).

Gable and Vivien Leigh in *Gone With the Wind*

No matter how much highbrow audiences might disparage *Gone With the Wind*, it is not difficult to understand the appeal that it continues to have on audiences. The sweeping, dramatic plot centers on the vain Scarlett O'Hara and her attempt to find a spouse. Set in the American South during the Civil War and the Reconstruction era, Leigh's southern belle encapsulates the decadence of the South in its declining state. Her character is simultaneously egotistical and unlikeable, but Scarlett also exudes just enough pathos to appeal to a wide audience. The film also benefits from having one of the most celebrated romantic pairings of all time, as Gable's Rhett Butler, a wild and wealthy Southern gentleman, is the ideal match for Scarlett O'Hara. Despite spanning nearly four hours in length, the baroque plot has an almost unmatched ability to captivate viewers.

It is easy to become enraptured by the sweeping plot and bravura formal stylings of the film, yet viewers should not cast a blind eye to the ideology of *Gone With the Wind*. In particular, the film displays a casual racism that was not uncommon in 1930s Hollywood yet cannot be brushed aside by 21st century viewers. The most flagrant example of racial inequality concerns Scarlett's relationship with her black servant, Mammy, who displays no interest in breaking free from her submissive condition. The film also contains discriminatory language, and while one could argue that it merely followed the material in the book, the failure to remove the racist underpinnings of the plot amounted to an implicit acceptance of the offensive subject matter.

Gone With the Wind was awarded with 10 Oscars at the 1940 Academy Awards, an achievement made all the more impressive when considering the competition it faced. It is no accident that 1939 is often considered the greatest year in Hollywood film history, as *The Wizard of Oz*, *Mr. Smith Goes to Washington*, *Ninotchka*, and *Young Mr. Lincoln* were also among the famous films released that year. However, the showering of awards, particularly the Academy Award given to Hattie McDaniel, sparked an outcry from the National Association for the Advancement of Colored People (NAACP). In response, McDaniel refused to criticize either her role or the film as a whole. Ultimately, the Academy Awards saga itself was indicative of how *Gone With the Wind* is a cherished American classic on the one hand, but also a film that has caused great outrage from a significant portion of American society.

For her part, critics praised Leigh's performance, with one *New York Times* review opining, "Miss Leigh's Scarlett has vindicated the absurd talent quest that indirectly turned her up. She is so perfectly designed for the part by art and nature that any other actress in the role would be inconceivable." Leigh won her first Oscar, the Academy Award for Best Actress, for her portrayal of Scarlett, and she also won the coveted New York Film Critics Circle Award for Best Actress. Of course, the film won her one other more dubious honor. For the rest of her life, she would be asked that eternal question, "Did Scarlett get Rhett back?" Her typical answer was somewhat cagey, "I'm not sure that Scarlett was a good enough person for Rhett, even at the end. And I doubt if he could ever have had a peaceful life with her. She had broken him down completely and really didn't repay him for it. I admire her – heaven knows – and only wish she could be happy. But – I don't know – one feels at the end that she can always take care of herself."

Meanwhile, Gable was now at the peak of his career, and he noticed the change that *Gone with the Wind* had on how people viewed him. He once noted, "Damn it. I never conceived of this. When I rode through Atlanta's streets today it wasn't like an opening at Grauman's Chinese at Hollywood. It wasn't like anything I ever experienced in my life. It was almost too big for me to take. And I hope to heaven when I leave here tomorrow night, after everybody has seen the picture, that I leave as Rhett Butler and not Clark Gable."

Chapter 6: World War II Years

"I don't want a lot of strangers looking down at my wrinkles and my big fat belly when I'm dead." – Clark Gable

Vivien in the early 1940s

"My first husband and I are still good friends and there is no earthly reason why I should not see him. Larry and I are very much in love." - Vivien Leigh

While playing Scarlett O'Hara made Vivien Leigh a star, it also put her in danger of being typecast, a concern she mentioned to a reporter: "If there is one thing I should object to, it is to become identified with one type of character. After all, anyone on the stage should be prepared to discard his own personality and assume that which the play calls for. That's half the fun of acting. An actress must be able to assume different dialects, accents, mannerisms and actions. When she walks out on the stage or before a camera she must be equipped to transform herself. No matter how much she must change her personality she must always seem natural. That is the hard part of the job." This may be one of the reasons why she returned to the stage following *Gone With the Wind*, feeling live productions were more challenging than films. She added, "The people of the theatre must be students. Even when they are acting they must be able to appraise what they are doing. I know there are stories about actors losing themselves in their parts, but good actors never do this. They must always be masters of themselves or they are not good actors. Yet a performance must not seem labored. The audience must receive the impression that the lines are being said for the first time."

In the spring of 1940, Leigh and Olivier used their own money to open Romeo and Juliet on Broadway. One might question why a 26 year old woman with a husband and child was playing opposite a 33 year old man as star-crossed teenage lovers, but this was not as big a problem for New York audiences as the pair's personal lives. While both received their longed for divorces just before they began the production, the press in New York made much of the fact that they had begun their affair while still married to others. Both actors had other things on their minds too. War had broken out in Europe, and Britain was under attack, so the two were under increasing pressure to return home and help with the war effort. Leigh commented to a reporter, "Everything seems so useless these days, and so unimportant. Even acting is inconsequential when one thinks of what is going on over there."

The critics also had a field day with the production, criticizing both the acting and the staging of the show. It closed early, causing a critical financial problem for both Leigh and Olivier. Leigh blamed the subject matter: "Despite the fact that they are constructed in many short scenes, too much in them depends on the actual words. While dialogue counts in the cinema, it is not the spoken word alone that carries a screen play. No matter how good a stage play may be, it must be rewritten for the screen, because while an audience may be enthralled for a long time while watching real people acting a scene, in the cinema there must be constant change to prevent monotony."

Despite the pressure, instead of returning to England, Leigh and Olivier decided to remain in America and get married. The wedding took place on August 31, 1940, in a quiet ceremony at a luxury resort in Santa Barbara, California. Their witnesses were Katherine Hepburn and Garson Kanin.

After completing work on a box office failure called *21 Days Together*, Leigh began her next big project in the fall of 1940, Waterloo Bridge. In it she played Myra, a dancer who became a prostitute after losing her job and believing her fiancé to be dead. Like so many of Leigh's movies, it ends tragically with Myra taking her own life. Told in flashbacks and set in then modern day England, it was meant to shore up British-American relations as the United States continued to hesitate on joining the war. A critic for the *New York Herald Tribune* wrote of Vivien in its review of the movie, "It is apparent, now, though, that her career is based on great talent and great beauty rather than on the supposed break she got when she was picked to play the most popular heroine of our day. Actually Gone With The Wind was extremely lucky to have her in it. Any film, or any stage work for that matter, is blessed by her participation. For here is an actress who combines all of the sorcery of a vivid personality with brilliant acting execution."

Leigh's next film, in which she once more starred with Olivier, was also meant to elicit sympathy for the war being fought by the British people against Hitler. Titled *That Hamilton Woman*, the movie told the true story of the love affair between British war hero Admiral Horatio Nelson and Lady Emma Hamilton. Like *Waterloo Bridge*, *That Hamilton Woman* is told in flashbacks as the imprisoned and aged Hamilton recalls her life. The film ends tragically with Hamilton alone and penniless after the death of Nelson, and when asked what happened after Nelson's death, Hamilton says, "There is no then. There is no after."

Olivier and Leigh in *That Hamilton Woman*

Not only was the film popular among American audiences, it was also a hit with the Soviet Union. Making the best of its popularity, Winston Churchill arranged for it to be viewed at a meeting of important foreign leaders, including President Franklin Roosevelt, and at the end of the movie he stood and solemnly intoned, "Gentlemen, I thought this film would interest you, showing great events similar to those in which you have just been taking part." Churchill later sent a note of thanks to the Oliviers for their work, and a friendship was born that would last for the rest of their lives.

Meanwhile, in the aftermath of *Gone With the Wind*, Gable continued to act at a prolific rate, but none of the films achieved any great success. His life remained quiet and comfortable until

January 1942, when he was suddenly widowed after Carole Lombard died in a plane crash. She and her mother had gone on a tour selling war bonds, and the plane crashed near Las Vegas. Lombard was the first female casualty to die as a result of World War II, and despite flying to the scene of the accident, there was nothing Gable could do to amend the tragedy. The death plunged him into a deep depression, and despite finishing the film in which he was acting at the time, *Somewhere I'll Find You* (1942), Gable was ultimately unable to mask his heartbreak and even lost 20 pounds. Actress Esther Williams pointed out that after Lombard's death, Gable "was never the same. His heart sank a bit."

During World War II, Hollywood studios made every effort to prevent their stars from enlisting, since actors were valuable commodities. Even if they emerged from combat without suffering any wounds, their time away from the studio still constituted a substantial financial loss. However, with his wife having just passed away, there was little resistance that MGM could justifiably make, and Gable enlisted in the Air Force, where he was first given a special assignment. Eventually, he progressed through the ranks and was appointed First Lieutenant. In 1943, he accompanied the 351st Bomb Group to England and was promoted to Captain, spending 1943 in England at the RAF Polebrook with the 351st Bomb Group. While there, he was involved in combat and eventually earned an Air Medal and Distinguished Flying Cross. The following year, he was appointed to the rank of Major, but he was relieved from active duty in June 1944. Even so, it was not until 1947 that he resigned his commission.

Gable in Britain in 1943

Gable and Jimmy Stewart during World War II

Despite reticence from the studios, it was not terribly unusual for actors to enlist in the service in some capacity. What distinguished Gable's experience in the Armed Forces from those of many of his peers in Hollywood is that he displayed a fierce commitment to progressing through the ranks and serving the country to his fullest capacity, even after (and perhaps because) his wife had lost her own life due to World War II. In many ways, serving his country constituted an entirely separate career for Gable, one that monopolized his time and attention for two years. When he returned, both his professional and personal lives were vastly different.

When the United States entered World War II after Pearl Harbor near the end of 1941, the Oliviers returned to England and didn't make any films during the war years. At first, they lived quietly in a little town outside London, relishing the time they were able to spend together when Olivier was not away serving with the British Navy. A friend described a poignant scene that seems now to have encompassed not only their lives at that moment, but also most of their years together: "At midnight we left them. London was blazing under the bombardments. All my life I will remember the frail silhouette of Vivien as she accompanied us under the porch roof, looking serious and serene, nestled in her husband's arms and illuminated by the reddish flashes that signaled that another 'V-1' had just destroyed another district in London."

Vivien went on a morale boosting tour in 1943, performing for the troops in North Africa, but it was during this patriotic mission that Leigh contracted the disease which would eventually take her life. It began with cold-like symptoms but persisted until it became a cough and fever that would not go away. The following year doctors determined that she had tuberculosis and hospitalized her for nearly a month while she recovered, but her condition was exacerbated by her heavy smoking, which was up to four packs a day.

Upon returning from the war, Gable still qualified as a major name in Hollywood, but his box office appeal was somewhat ambiguous; he had been away from the camera for three full years, and he was also in his mid-40s. Gable's first film after returning was *Adventure* (1945), a relatively minor romantic comedy that paired him with Greer Garson and featured the memorable publicity slogan "Gable's back and Garson's got him." The film is not well-remembered, and it was Gable's activity off the movie set garnered more headlines. In 1944, he joined the Motion Picture Alliance for the Preservation of American ideals, an organization housing many of Hollywood's more conservative figures. In joining the organization, Gable distanced himself early on from any allegations that may have otherwise been directed toward him during the Red Scare that subsumed Hollywood in the years to come.

During the late 1940s, Gable's romantic pursuits continued to generate publicity. He and Joan Crawford, who had been involved in an affair early in Clark's career, were once again romantically involved. The relationship did not last, and Gable then began seeing Sylvia Ashley, an actress and model from Britain. Ashley was well-known for having been the widow of screen legend Douglas Fairbanks, at least until she and Gable married in 1949. Three years younger than Clark, the age dynamics of the relationship more closely resembled Gable's third marriage than his first two. Despite being more age-compatible than either of Gable's first two wives, however, the marriage with Ashley was doomed to fail. After three years together, they obtained a divorce, and by 1952, Gable was once again single.

as soon as the war ended in 1945, Leigh and Olivier returned to the screen together, this time playing the title roles in *Caesar and Cleopatra*. Though she was beautiful as the doomed queen who loved too much, Leigh's performance was not well received and the movie made little money.

During filming, Vivien learned that she was pregnant, but despite being thrilled to have Olivier's baby, she was devastated when she later miscarried. She became clinically depressed, spending her days alternating between sobbing and screaming, until she ultimately suffered a complete breakdown, attacking Olivier and pounding on him with her fists until she collapsed in a heap at his feet. By this time, Olivier had developed the ability to read his troubled wife's moods, and he was aware that when she became increasingly hyperactive and stopped sleeping, a blowup and breakdown were on the horizon.

Perhaps hoping that a stage schedule would be easier for her to keep, Olivier arranged for Leigh to play opposite him in *The Skin of Our Teeth* in London. This play, written by Thornton

Wilder, tells the story of mankind across time, and though set in the modern era of the late 1940s, it attempted to tell tales from many ancient eras of history. The play did well and was more successful than their previous efforts with Romeo and Juliet. Furthermore, in 1947, Olivier received a knighthood from King George VI in recognition of his work on stage and on behalf of the war effort. Upon his receiving his title, Vivien herself became Lady Olivier.

After that, Vivien returned to work on her next picture, based off Leo Tolstoy's *Anna Karenina*. Almost a cross between *Waterloo Bridge* and *That Hamilton Woman*, Leigh played the title role as yet another mistress who, upon losing her lover, decides to commit suicide. *Anna Karenina* did not do well at the box office, nor was it liked by the critics of the day, but Vivien and Olivier quickly took a six month tour to raise funds for the Old Vic Theatre in London. Olivier served on the board of the theatre and may have thought that a change of scenery would do the increasingly high-strung Leigh some good. At first, all went well as they made their way south to Australia and then New Zealand. He did some Shakespeare, and the two of them appeared together in *The School for Scandal* by Richard Sheridan. The press especially loved meeting Leigh in person, and she was able to charm her way into their hearts again and again, but sadly, as the tour wore on, Leigh had trouble sleeping, going into a manic phase that resulted in her refusing to go on stage in Christchurch, New Zealand. Losing his temper, Olivier slapped her face, and she then slapped him back and cursed at him before finally calming down and beginning her performance. Olivier would later believe that he first "lost Vivien" in Australia, which may very well be true since, in addition to becoming increasingly irrational, Leigh also started an affair with actor Peter Finch while in Australia. The affair would last for several years, and they covered their tracks so well that Olivier actually considered the young man one of his best friends.

Peter Finch

Upon returning to London, the Oliviers took the shows that they had been doing and recombined them into a production for the West End of London. This production only lasted a few months, however, before Leigh was again chosen to play a tragic Southern belle, the miserable Blanche DuBois in *A Streetcar Named Desire*.

Chapter 7: Blanche DuBois

Vivien Leigh in the trailer for *A Streetcar Named Desire*

"A lucky thing Eva Peron was. She died at 32. I'm already 45." – Vivien Leigh

"Scorpios burn themselves out and eat themselves up and they are careless about themselves - like me. I swing between happiness and misery and I cry easily. I am a mixture of my mother's determination and my father's optimism. I am part prude and part non-conformist and I say what I think and don't dissemble. I am a mixture of French, Irish and Yorkshire, and perhaps that's what it all is." - Vivien Leigh

Many people have speculated over why Vivien Leigh wanted to play Blanche DuBois in *A Streetcar Named Desire* so much. Some have wondered if, by returning to the persona of a Southern belle, she might have been looking to regain some of the glory and attention she enjoyed as Scarlett O'Hara. Others have posited that the role of an aging beauty plagued by madness might have appealed to her troubled mind, and she had made her reputation as an actress specializing in works that had unhappy endings. Finally, many believe that she wanted the role for the same reason she wanted to be Scarlett: to secure the best role available to her at the time.

Again, just as she had with *Gone With the Wind*, Leigh had a certain advantage over many of the other actresses vying for the role. She knew the show's producer, Irene Mayer Selznick (David Selznick's daughter-in-law), from her days in Hollywood, and Irene had seen Leigh in both *The School for Scandal* and *Antigone* and believed Vivien would be excellent in the role. She also hired Olivier to direct the production, putting him in the unusual position of being his wife's boss.

When the play opened in London's West End in 1949, it had a large audience but earned small praise from the critics. Much to both of the Oliviers' embarrassment, many of the people who came to see the play were attracted by its more controversial elements, including references to promiscuity and homosexuality, as well as a scene of implied rape. The media fed this interest by making much of the scandalous nature of the play, but the critics were not so helpful. Once again, they criticized Leigh's soft voice for being difficult to understand. One man did support their efforts, however. Noel Coward publicly praised both the play and Leigh's performance in it.

Regardless of critical acclaim, the play ended up being quite popular and ran for more than 300 performances. Meanwhile, Broadway had a version as well. Elia Kazan, known for his work at the Group Theatre, was slated to direct Tennessee Williams' classic on Broadway, and after *Truckline Café*, he was intent on having a young actor named Marlon Brando playing the role of Stanley Kowalski, the brutish, outwardly sexual brother-in-law of the main character, Blanche DuBois, the fragile, alcoholic, guilt-ridden Southern belle that the playwright based on himself. Producer Irene Selznick was set to cast John Garfield or Burt Lancaster in the role of Stanley, but Brando personally campaigned for the role, resulting in Kazan giving him carfare to Provincetown, Massachusetts to audition for Williams. It was an impressive reading, and the playwright was convinced that the production had found its Stanley. Kazan convinced Selznick to cast Brando, while Jessica Tandy, after her role in Williams' one act *Portrait of a Madonna,* was cast as Blanche.

Kazan

Tennessee Williams

A Streetcar Named Desire is the story of an aging vestige of the gentility of the Old South. Blanche DuBois is a repressed yet delusional woman who is trapped by her own desperate attempts to cling to her youth, physical attractiveness and sexuality. The play intends to follow her descent into madness, partially due to her callous, cruel and ultimately violent treatment by Stanley. But soon after rehearsals began, it became more than apparent that a shift had occurred, and the focus of the play surrendered to the power of Brando's interpretation of Stanley. A force of nature himself, Brando basically wrestled the focus of the play from the hands of Tandy, making it Stanley's story, not Blanche's. *Streetcar* opened in 1947, and Brando's performance was hailed as a landmark theatrical event. His Kowalski was unprecedented as a man of irresistible sexuality and frightening violence, one who simultaneously used his animal appeal to conquer and manipulate his wife Stella and terrorize his sister-in-law Blanche.

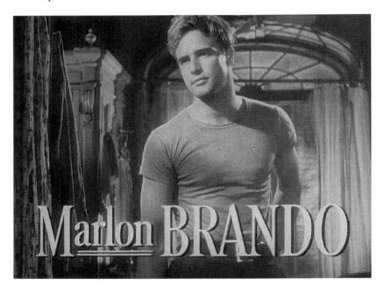

Screenshot of Brando from the trailer for the film A Streetcar Named Desire

Naturally, by the time the stage performances were over, Hollywood wanted to make a movie. Leigh had been chosen to bring her character to the big screen. While she got along well with her co-star, Marlon Brando, she found director Elia Kazan difficult to work with. Their "love/hate relationship" was best summed up in his public evaluation of her performance: "She had a small talent but, as work progressed, I became full of admiration for the greatest determination to excel of any actress I've known. She'd have crawled over broken glass if she thought it would help her performance. In the scenes that counted, she excelled." For her part, Leigh found working in pictures again exhausting and told one reporter: "I had nine months in the theatre of Blanche DuBois. Now she's in command of me." Perhaps the only thing that saved her from a complete meltdown was the fact the Olivier had gone with her to Hollywood to star in another film, and he noted, "Vivien was too much affected by the parts she played...it had a great deal to do with playing Blanche DuBois being ill in the same way."

Nevertheless, in the end, Leigh's performance in A Streetcar Named Desire was the crowning achievement of her career. Although sanitized to accommodate the Hays Code restrictions, the film set Hollywood on fire and shot Brando's career into the stratosphere. Brando was thrilled that Vivien replaced Tandy because he always thought that Tandy was shrill, an attribute which encouraged the audience to side with Stanley. He thought Leigh was ideal, as she was not only a great beauty but she, like Blanche, was a troubled soul in her real life, battling ongoing mental illness. Thus, her performance came much closer than Tandy's to his own in its depth, indelibility and complexity. She won another Academy Award for Best Actress, another New York Film Critics Circle Award for Best Actress and her only British Academy of Film and Television Arts (BAFTA) Award for Best British Actress. Tennessee Williams himself would later say that Leigh's Blanche DuBois was "everything that I intended, and much that I had never dreamed of."

Sadly, Blanche DuBois cost Leigh more than any other character she had ever played, as she later claimed that playing Blanche "tipped me over into madness." Brando concurred, writing in his autobiography, "In many ways she was Blanche. She was memorably beautiful, one of the great beauties of the screen, but she was also vulnerable, and her own life had been very much like that of Tennessee's wounded butterfly."

Chapter 8: Clark Gable's Final Years

The late 1940s and early 1950s were bittersweet for Gable's career. On the one hand, he continued to secure major acting roles, but he found his opportunities less than fulfilling. One of his most significant post-war films was *The Hucksters* (1947), which paired him with Ava Gardner for the first time, although Deborah Kerr served as his chief co-star for the film. In the film, Gable plays a wealthy man who returns from World War II with the ambition of earning a fortune. He discards all of his money and works his way up the socioeconomic ladder from square one. The film has a parallel between that main plot and the romantic plot, in which he must similarly prove his worthiness to Kay (Deborah Kerr), the socialite with whom he falls in love. The film received lukewarm reviews but did lead to two additional films starring both Gable and Ava Gardner: *Lone Star* (1952) and *Mogambo* (1953). The latter film is particularly noteworthy, as it remade *Red Dust*, one of Gable's earliest films. The film, which not only co-starred Ava Gardner but also Grace Kelly, was directed by John Ford. With such a famous cast and an acclaimed director, the public was understandably optimistic, but it is now almost entirely forgotten. The adventurous plot, set in Africa, was full of novelty, but the relatively thin narrative kept it from becoming a classic.

Gable and Ava Gardner in *The Hucksters*

Gable began to grow frustrated with the roles that were made available to him, and in 1953 he decided against renewing his contract. This decision wasn't unusual, because by 1953 it was a common practice for major stars to operate as independent contractors. What made Clark's case different from that of other stars, like Cary Grant, is that the lack of appealing opportunities was more a reflection of his age and status within the industry. Simply put, he was in the process of slipping from the list of most marketable stars in Hollywood.

His next major career move came in 1955, when he and Jane Russell founded a production company together. The first and only film produced by Gable was *The King and Four Queens* (1956), which was directed by the famous Raoul Walsh and co-starred Jane Powell. Despite being nearly 55 years old at the time of filming, Gable starred in the action film, playing the role of a cowboy who romances a group of widows (and their mother-in-law) in the hopes of inheriting their fortune. By this point in his career, Gable was hardly up to the task of playing an action hero, but the comedic elements of the plot supplied his performance with an irony that makes the film somewhat tongue-in-cheek in its treatment of Clark's masculinity. At the same time, producing the film was so taxing that Gable would not produce another film.

As the 1950s progressed, Gable's health began to deteriorate, and his career slowed down as well. Between 1956 and 1961, he averaged just one film per year. In 1958, Gable fully admitted,

"My days of playing the dashing lover are over. I'm no longer believable in those parts. There has been considerable talk about older guys wooing and winning leading ladies half their age. I don't think the public likes it, and I don't care for it myself. It's not realistic. Actresses that I started out with like Joan Crawford and Barbara Stanwyck have long since quit playing glamour girls and sweet young things. Now it's time I acted my age. Let's be honest. It's a character role, and I'll be playing more of them. There's a risk involved, of course. I have no idea if I can attain the success as a character actor as I did playing the dashing young lover, but it's a chance I have to take. Not everybody is able to do it."

His life off the movie set began to settle down as well when he married Kay Spreckels, a former fashion model and actress who he had known for years. In fact, their first date had taken place over a decade before they were married, and it ended up with Gable botching an attempt to cook dinner for her at his ranch. When an accident left them both covered in gravy, Gable said to her, "Well, the first date you have with me and you end up in the gravy; at least you won't forget it. I imagine I've made quite the impression on you."

Like Gable, Spreckels had already been married a number of times, but she and Clark had a strong rapport, and their marriage was successful. She later said of him, "Looking back I wonder if there are many people who even in 25 or 30 years of marriage find the happiness that Clark and I had in those five years and four months." She also added, "Sometimes I would try to tease Clark into telling me some tasty morsels about his former leading ladies, but I might as well have banged my head against a stone wall. He simply refused to gossip. He'd break into that schoolboy grin that I found so irresistible and say, 'She's a fine girl. A fine girl.' That's the only thing I didn't like about my remarkable husband, for I'm a gal who likes a bit of gossip, now and then."

Kay Spreckels

By the end of the decade, Gable began showing his age. On the movie set, he struggled to hold his posture, particularly during long takes, and his weight also ballooned. In an effort to hide his escalating weight, his 1958 film *Teacher's Pet* was filmed in black-and-white, but even with the cosmetic tactics, it was impossible not to notice that Gable was losing his athleticism and virility. In response to this, he began to shift away from roles that demanded great physicality and shifted toward more comedic parts. One such film, *It Started in Naples* (1960), received strong reviews and was even nominated for an Academy Award for Best Art Direction. The romantic comedic plot paired Gable with Sophia Loren, with Clark playing the role of an American lawyer and Loren an Italian nightclub singer. The lighthearted film cast Gable in a charming light without demanding the physical prowess of his earlier performances.

Clark Gable's final film, *The Misfits*, was the most notable of his final years, especially because it included Marilyn Monroe and her husband, Arthur Miller. Monroe had long fantasized about Clark Gable, even going so far as to tell people that he was her father, and Miller wrote the script for the film specifically with Monroe in mind (Taraborelli). The movie was made when their marriage was in a state of disarray, and Monroe's life as a whole had already begun the downward spiral that culminated with her death in 1962. As the title suggests, the film casts each of the characters in a less than favorable light. Monroe stars as Roslyn Tabor, a divorcee who becomes romantically involved with Gable's character, an aging cowboy named Gay Langland. The plot mainly consists of the rowdy exploits of the main characters, whose reckless behavior masks a deep underlying ennui.

The Misfits is not only remembered for its famous cast but also for the subtext surrounding the cast. The film serve as a meta-commentary on Monroe's lifelong infatuation with Clark Gable, and Montgomery Clift's performance as a jaded rodeo performer makes reference to Clift's own personal insecurities. Far from a traditional Western with a macho hero, the film instead adopts a mood of alienation and discontent, leading Georgiana Banita to characterize it as the rare Western with an absent image of patriarchy.

Furthermore, the somber plot was mirrored with a difficult production that taxed everyone involved. Naturally, Monroe had caught Gable's eye, and he said of her, "Everything Marilyn does is different from any other woman, strange and exciting, from the way she talks to the way she uses that magnificent torso." But by 1961, Monroe was heavily addicted to sleeping pills, and her sporadic attendance kept everyone irritable. Gable himself complained, "The title sums up this mess. Miller, Monroe and Clift - they don't know what the hell they're doing. We don't belong in the same room together."

Even worse, the production took a great toll on Gable, whose health quickly deteriorated as he began suffering from a heart condition. It is possible that his heart condition was exacerbated by an extreme diet he took in order to lose weight and attempt to transform his body into proper physical condition for the role, and it didn't help that Gable actually insisted on performing his own stunts, one of which involved being dragged hundreds of feet. Whatever the cause, Gable's health took a sharp turn for the worse during the making of the film, and when he died on November 16, 1960 from the effects of a severe heart attack, the film had not yet been completed.

Although his death was undeniably untimely, Lesley Brill notes that the off-screen drama of *The Misfits* was appropriately suited to the tragedy of the actors involved: "Made in the midst of 'real life dramas,' *The Misfits* undertakes an imaginative exploration of pain and change and death. If the circumstances surrounding its production do not finally affect the images and words of the movie itself, they nonetheless attach to it an aura of tragic richness as an avatar of its ill-fated cast. The biographies of its makers resonate forlornly with the sadness of much of its story." (76).

Given the star-crossed fate of the cast members, *The Misfits* film remains a film of great sadness, one that put an abrupt end to Clark Gable's life and imbued the narrative with an overarching melancholy. The tragedy of Gable's death was made all the more pronounced by the fact that Gable's wife, Kay, gave birth to their son just months after his death.

Clark Gable will forever be best known for starring in *Gone With the Wind*, a film that is firmly entrenched within the canon of American film classics and arguably the most beloved film ever made. The fact Gable starred in such a well-loved film reflects his status as a screen legend of the first order, but it is also important to remember that he displayed great ability in other films as well. In fact, his lone Academy Award victory came not for *Gone With the Wind* but in recognition of his performance in *It Happened One Night*. In an age in which Hollywood was dominated by gangster heroes on the one hand and screwball comedy and musical actors on the other, Gable was able to combine rugged masculinity with refined sophistication in a way that was truly unprecedented. If he was, for a brief period, more popular than either Cary Grant (the romantic comedy actor par excellence) or Gary Cooper (premier action hero), it is not because he beat them at their own game but because he was able to combine the two. As Doris Day put it, "He was as masculine as any man I've ever known, and as much a little boy as a grown man could be – it was this combination that had such a devastating effect on women."

At the same time, the sophisticated veneer of Clark Gable's career masked a life filled with persistent tragedy. His mother and stepmother both died when he was young, and the death of Carole Lombard magnifies how even after reaching stardom, Gable's life continued to involve deep sorrow. Having died just before his 60th birthday, Gable was denied a chance at old age, and he seemed poised to transition to a life of quiet domesticity, with his acting career nearing its end and a new existence as a father on the horizon. Had he lived longer, it is unlikely that his career would have taken new directions. The tragedy of his death lies not so much in lost career opportunities but rather in the fact that Gable was denied the chance to raise a family.

Even though he died before he retired, it is impossible to deny that Clark Gable had a pronounced effect on Hollywood film history. In the throes of the Great Depression, he offered a hero that male and female viewers alike could identify with, displaying an acting style that was highly athletic yet at the same time very genteel. It is no accident that women like Marilyn Monroe fantasized over him; he was the ideal model for an upstanding American gentleman and comported himself seemingly without flaw. Even after returning from World War II and entering his late career, Gable offered a level of charm that few could match, and despite dying prematurely, his ability to continue starring in films even as he approached old age attested to his popularity. Still, it will always be the 1930s films, particularly *It Happened One Night* and *Gone with the Wind*, that dominate discussions of Clark Gable, who will forever be recognized as one of the titans of Hollywood's Golden Age.

Chapter 9: Vivien Leigh's Final Years

Leigh and Olivier returned to the stage together in 1951, playing the title roles in Shakespeare's *Antony and Cleopatra* and George Bernard Shaw's *Caesar and Cleopatra*, but this time they created an unusual arrangement. Instead of launching one play and seeing it to completion before beginning the next, they ran the two performances simultaneously, staging each on alternate nights. The formula worked, and both productions were so well received that after a successful run in London, they opened both plays on Broadway in 1952. Again, most of the reviews were positive, but there was one tough critic for Vivien Leigh as Cleopatra I the form of Kenneth Tynan, who not only criticized her performance but speculated that her poor acting was even having a negative effect of Olivier's career. This was almost more than the fragile Leigh could handle. She began to obsess on his words, ignoring all the positive reviews given by other critics, and she drove herself harder and harder to succeed, never satisfied that she was doing a good enough job. By the time the play closed in late 1952, she was both physically and mentally exhausted.

To make matters worse, Leigh jumped right in to a new film, *Elephant Walk*, which was filmed on location in Ceylon (now Sri Lanka) and starred Peter Finch as Leigh's husband. The heat and the strange country, not to mention playing opposite of her lover, proved to be too much for Vivien, who suffered a full-scale nervous breakdown. Olivier travelled to Ceylon to bring her home and settled her quietly into Netherne Hospital, in Surrey. Although it was one of the best psychiatric hospitals in England, it was insufficient for her level of derangement, so Olivier had her moved to University College Hospital in London. She was then given electro-convulsive therapy, considered the best treatment option at the time.

Sadly, the therapies did not work for Leigh. Instead of getting better, she drifted in and out of coherent thought, sometimes sobbing hysterically, other times laughing at nothing. During this period, she told Olivier about her affair with Finch and declared that she was in love with him, but since he was more concerned about her health than his own feelings, Olivier continued to nurse her and protect her from prying eyes over the months it took her to recover. By the time she was released from the hospital, Leigh was determined never to allow herself to be admitted to a mental health facility again.

By 1953, Leigh had broken off her affair with Finch and had recovered sufficiently to return to the stage, starring with Olivier in *The Sleeping Prince*. After a moderately successful run with that play, they opened together at Stratford-Upon-Avon in 1953. Returning to their Shakespearean roots, they starred together first in *Twelfth Night*, then in *Macbeth*, and finally in *Titus Andronicus*. The public was thrilled to see the two sharing the stage again and they played to packed houses night after night. Leigh basked in the light of the success, even though she sometimes struggled with the director, the famous actor John Gielgud. Part of the problem was Olivier's own protective nature. Gielgud complained of this in a letter to a friend in April of 1955: "….perhaps I may still make a good thing of that divine play, especially if he [Olivier] will let me pull her little ladyship [Leigh] (who is brainier than he is but not a born actress) out of her timidity and safeness. He dares too confidently (and will always carry an undiscriminating audience with him) while she hardly dares at all and is terrified of overreaching her technique and doing anything that she has not killed the spontaneity of by over practice."

Leigh made several movies in the late 1950s and early 1960s but none of them are memorable. In the first, 1955's *The Deep Blue Sea*, she played opposite Kenneth More, who openly agreed with the critics that the two did not really connect on screen. She also starred in the title role of the *The Roman Spring of Mrs. Stone* in 1961 and in *Ship of Fools* in 1965. Noel Coward wanted

Leigh for *South Sea Bubble* but she became pregnant again shortly after they began filming. 43 years old and concerned about her health, she dropped out of the picture, but this pregnancy also ended in a miscarriage, again sending her spiraling down into a depression.

Vivien in *The Deep Blue Sea*

In hopes of snapping out of her sadness, she traveled to Europe to tour with Olivier in *Titus Andronicus*, but she was still very moody and given to fits of rage against Olivier and the other actors. He again took her home to England and enlisted the help of Leigh Holman, Vivian's first husband, to calm her down. Holman and Leigh had remained friends, and he often seemed to be the only one who could calm her when she was out of control, but neither man, nor the two of them working together, was strong enough to bring Leigh back from the darkness this time.

Like many bipolar people, Leigh struggled with promiscuity, which has led some biographers to label her a nymphomaniac, but this is not a fair evaluation of her behavior. She did take on a number of lovers, but she was not indiscriminate with whom she slept. In 1958, full of guilt over all that she had put both her husbands through and yet unable to control much of her behavior, she began what would be her final relationship. She began an affair with fellow actor Jack Merivale. Olivier, worn out from trying to care for her, was satisfied to let her go, especially after Merivale contacted him and assured him that he understood her mental frailty and would take good care of her. As much as it must have hurt him when the two divorced in 1960, it must have been something of a relief too. He would later recall, "Throughout her possession by that uncannily evil monster, manic depression, with its deadly ever-tightening spirals, she retained her own individual canniness – an ability to disguise her true mental condition from almost all except me, for whom she could hardly be expected to take the trouble." She later admitted she never stopped loving Olivier, stating, "I would rather have lived a short life with Larry than face a long one without him."

Vivien and Merivale

Thankfully, Merivale was good for Leigh, and in 1959, she enjoyed a short lived revival in her career as she got to play a comedic role in Noel Coward's *Look After Lulu*. The critics spoke well of the production, and it seemed for a while that her career might be on the rise. However, that same year, Leigh suffered another critical loss when her close friend, Kay Kendall, died at the age of 33. Leigh, speaking at her funeral, read from a speech written for her by well-known playwright Terence Rattigan: "It was as if she had a premonition that the gift of life which she relished so greatly would not be hers for very long - with such intensity and gaiety and fervor did she pack every minute of her stay on earth. Rest and Peace were two things that in life Kay hardly knew. They would have seemed a waste of time". The same might just as easily have been said about Leigh herself.

In July 1961, Merivale took Leigh on a yearlong tour around the world, and she performed everywhere from Australia to South America. Still as beautiful as ever, she wowed audiences in every land, and it was the first time she had ever made her own way on stage without Olivier around to help her. In 1963 she won her first Tony Award, snaring the Tony for Best Actress in a Musical for her performance in Tovarich.

In May 1967, Leigh began work on A Delicate Balance, but early on during filming, she began to cough and run low grade fevers. The doctors diagnosed a recurrence of her tuberculosis and suggested she be hospitalized, but Leigh refused and instead went home to rest. Ensconced in her exquisite bedroom, she spent her days writing letters and enjoying visits with old friends. After several weeks in bed, she appeared to be recovering, but just after midnight on July 7, 1967, Merivale found her on the floor crumpled by their bed. He tried to revive her but she was dead, her lungs filled with fluid that she had been too weak to cough up. He immediately called their family doctor and several close friends to be with him. The doctor pronounced Leigh dead, and Merivale gently laid her body back in the bed. Then, when morning came, he placed a call to Laurence Olivier, himself in the hospital undergoing treatment for prostate cancer. Leaving his own sick bed, Olivier went immediately to the house. He would later write about that night, "I stood and prayed for forgiveness for all the evils that had sprung up between us. It has always been impossible for me not to believe that I was somehow the cause of Vivien's disturbances."

By this time, Merivale had contacted Leigh's mother and daughter (her father had died eight years earlier), and the two women flew to Hollywood, where they identified the body and began making funeral arrangements. A requiem mass for Leigh was held at St. Mary's Roman Catholic Church on July 12 at 10:00 in the morning. In a strange twist of fate, Cecil Tennant, Vivien's agent, died in an automobile accident on his way home from her funeral. She used to tell Tennant, "I will take you with me when I go."

Following the mass, Leigh's body was then taken to chapel of Golder's Green Crematorium in London, where she lay in state surrounded by white roses from Leigh's own garden. On August 15, a large memorial service was held at St. Martin-in-the-Fields Church in London's Trafalgar Square. After a brief prayer service, British actor Emlyn Williams read from "Of the Progresse of the Soule" by John Donne. Then John Gielgud gave a heartfelt eulogy that included this tribute: "To talk of Vivien Leigh in public so soon after her death is almost unbearable difficult for me...What seems to me most remarkable, as for as her career was concerned, was her steady determination to be a fine stage actress, to make her career in the living theatre, when, with her natural beauty, skill, and grace of movement, gifts which were of course invaluable in helping to create the magic of her personality, she could so easily have stayed aloof and supreme in her unique position as a screen actress." In addition to eulogies by Gielgud and others, the service featured clips from her most famous movies. And thus, friends said goodbye, not just to the troubled actress but to the saucy young belle, the Egyptian queen and the tormented fading southern beauty.

On October 8, Merivale, Holman, her mother and daughter all met together to scatter her ashes on the surface of a small lake at her country estate, Tickerage Mill, outside of Blackboys in East Sussex. And in the weeks and months following Leigh's death, memorials and tributes to her poured in from around the world. One of the first was given by the London Theatre District, who dimmed their lights for an hour in honor of their fallen compatriot. On March 17, 1968, Hollywood staged its own massive tribute to Leigh. Held at the University of Southern California, it was called "An Appreciation of Vivien Leigh" and featured screenings of the screen tests she had made for *Gone With the Wind.* On November 5, 1969, a plaque in her honor was placed on the wall of "the actor's church," St. Paul's Church in Convent Garden. In addition to her name and dates of birth and death, it features this quote from Antony and Cleopatra, "Now boast thee, death, in thy possession lies a lass unparallel'd".

Throughout her life, Leigh enjoyed giving gifts. In her will, she bequeathed something so personal that it was hard to believe. She left her lovely corneas, Scarlett's eyes that looked into Rhett's, Blanche's eyes that shied away from Stanley's, to science. Sadly, because of her tuberculosis, they couldn't be used. Leigh left most of her worldly wealth to her daughter, Suzanne Farrington. While she knew that she had never been a good mother to the girl in her youth, the two had reconciled during the last decade of Leigh's life and had enjoyed a warm relationship during that time. Suzanne had three boys, leading Leigh to once say, I've been a godmother loads of times, but being a grandmother is better than anything."

Honors continued to pour in for Vivien Leigh decades after her death. In 1985, she was chosen to appear on a series of postage stamps issued in the United Kingdom. In addition to Leigh, these stamps commemorated famous English screen legends Alfred Hitchcock, Peter Sellers, Charlie Chaplin and David Niven. Another set of stamps were issued in April 2013 to mark the 100th anniversary of her birth, a particularly unique tribute since she became one of the few non-royals to appear on more than one set of stamps.

Bibliography

Banita, Georgiana. "Re-Visioning the Western: Landscape and Gender in *The Misfits.*" *John Huston: Essays on a Restless Director*. Eds. Tony Tracy and Roddy Flynn. Jefferson: McFarland & Company, 2010. 94-110. Print.

Bean, Kendra and Claire Bloom. Vivien Leigh: An Intimate Portrait (2013)

Bret, David. *Clark Gable: Tormented Star*. Cambridge: Da Capo Press, 2008. Print.

Brill, Lesley. *John Huston's Filmmaking*. Cambridge: Cambridge University Press, 1997. Print.

DiLeo, John. Vivien Leigh (2011)

Edwards, Anne. Vivien Leigh: A Biography (2013)

Harris, Warren G. *Clark Gable: A Biography*. New York: Three Rivers Press, 2005. Print.

Haskell, Molly. *Frankly, My Dear: Gone With the Wind Revisited*. New Haven: Yale University Press, 2010. Print.

Lasky, Jesse L. Jr. and Pat Silver. Love Scene: The Story of Laurence Olivier and Vivien Leigh (1978)

Mizejewski, Linda. *It Happened One Night*. United Kingdom: John Wiley & Sons Ltd, 2010. Print.

Porter, Dawin and Roy Moseley. Damn You, Scarlett O'Hara: The Private Lives of Vivien Leigh and Laurence Olivier (2011)

Spicer, Christopher J. *Clark Gable: Biography, Filmography, Bibliography*. Jefferson: McFarland & Company, 2002. Print.

Taraborelli, J. Randy. *The Secret Life of Marilyn Monroe*. New York: Grand Central Publishing, 2009. Print.

Taylor, Helen. *Scarlett's Women: Gone With the Wind and Its Female Fans*. United Kingdom: Virago Press Limited, 1989. Print.

Vertrees, Alan David. *Selznick's Vision: Gone With the Wind and Hollywood Filmmaking*. Austin: University of Texas, 1997. Print.

Vickers, Hugo. Vivien Leigh: A Biography (1989)

Walker, Alexander. Vivien: The Life of Vivien Leigh (1994)

Made in the USA
Lexington, KY
11 August 2019